Plural policing

The mixed economy of visible patrols in England and Wales

Adam Crawford, Stuart Lister,

Sarah Blackburn and Jonathan Burnett

The
Nuffield
Foundation
1943–2003

First published in Great Britain in March 2005 by The Policy Press

The Policy Press
University of Bristol
Fourth Floor, Beacon House
Queen's Road
Bristol BS8 1QU
UK

Tel no +44 (0)117 331 4054
Fax no +44 (0)117 331 4093
E-mail tpp-info@bristol.ac.uk
www.policypress.org.uk

ISBN 1 86134 671 9

British Library Cataloguing in Publication Data
A catalogue record for this report is available from the British Library.

Library of Congress Cataloging-in-Publication Data
A catalog record for this report has been requested.

Cover design by Qube Design Associates, Bristol
Printed in Great Britain by MPG Books, Bodmin

Contents

List of tables and figures

Table

Figures

Acknowledgements

The research outlined in this report was generously funded by the Nuffield Foundation and significantly benefited from the support and encouragement provided throughout by Sharon Witherspoon and her colleagues. The report also draws on insights and understandings developed in the course of a number of parallel research projects funded by the Joseph Rowntree Foundation and West Yorkshire Police. We are particularly grateful to Lord Richard Best and Pat Kneen at the Joseph Rowntree Foundation and to Colin Cramphorn and Grahame Bullock of West Yorkshire Police.

We are much indebted to a large number of people in the various research sites. In particular, we would like to thank the following for their assistance and support: Jane Mills, Andy Pollard, Malachi Rangecroft, Imran Rehman and Shaun Tunstall in Bradford; Terry Atkinson, Steve Barron, Ralph Logan, Norman Milnes and Alan Parks in Gateshead; Neil Bowden, Eric Bowen, Paul King and Andy Mills in Leeds; Helen Cooney, Tony Jopson, Paul Rice and Ian Shannon in Liverpool; Paul Berry, Nigel Brown, Steve McKinney, George Mensah and David Ryder in Trafford Park; and Cindy Beaton, John Cook, Ian Crawford, Shelia Fletcher, Howard Harding, Bob Mowat and Jane Mowat in York.

Members of the Advisory Board (see Appendix B) have been a continual source of support, information and advice. Not only did they give up their valuable time to attend Advisory Board meetings and comment on papers circulated and a draft report, but also many of them kindly agreed to be interviewed or provided written documentation in the course of the research. Some of the initial findings presented in this report were first presented at a one-day conference on 28 October 2004, which was generously supported by the Nuffield Foundation and the Advisory Board members. We are particularly grateful to Louise Bennett, Sir Ian Blair, Richard Childs, David Dickinson, Mike Fagan, Margaret Geary, Mark Gore, Peter Hermitage, Mike Hough, Anunay Jha, Mark Liddle, Molly Meacher, Tim Newburn, Peter Neyroud, Les Parrett, Robert Reiner, Lawrence Springall, Jaap de Waard, Frank Warburton and Carole Willis. In addition, a number of other people have assisted and contributed to the insights provided in this report, including Gavin Butler, Mark Button, Don Crabtree, Jeremy Crump, Peter Davies, Martin Innes, Les Johnston, Ian Loader, Martin Mitchell, Clifford Shearing and Lawrence Singer.

As ever, Tim Newburn has been an ongoing source of inspiration and insight. We are also grateful to Mike Hough who encouraged us to publish the study's findings in this exciting new *Researching Criminal Justice* series for The Policy Press.

Finally, we would like to thank Peter Shepherd for assistance with some of the data collection and geographic mapping. Both Sally Pearson and Kathryn Munn worked as research officers on the Nuffield and Joseph Rowntree Foundation reports and contributed to the data collection in the early stages of the research. Nicki Stick assisted with data inputting as well as conducting some of public reception surveys along with Christopher Carney and David Curtis, for which we are grateful. Susan Flint has tirelessly proofread and commented on various versions of the typescript.

Summary

Modern policing in a changing world faces many challenges, few more pressing than responding adequately to public demands for more, and more visible, security personnel. Feelings about local safety and well-being are influenced by wider, global insecurities and generic risks. Concerns about declining respect for authority, waning public institutions and intermediaries and the degradation of the urban environment by low-level incivilities have all left the public searching for solutions to local anxieties about crime and anti-social behaviour. Meeting public perceptions of insecurity has become a central component in contemporary planning, service provision and urban regeneration. At the same time, businesses, organisations and the public have increasingly lost confidence in the capacity of the police to deliver community-based and locally tied patrol officers as part of routine police provision and have begun to experiment with diverse forms of additional security.

We stand at the dawn of a fundamental shift in the way in which public and quasi-public places are policed, with significant implications for styles of policing, community engagement, civic renewal, social inclusion and citizenship. The emerging mixed economy of visible security patrols raises fundamental questions concerning the challenges of coordination, the future role of the public police, relations between policing personnel and those they serve, as well as regarding the accountability, governance and regulation of this mixed economy.

- There is now an established mixed economy of visible security patrols incorporating a range of sworn police officers, special constables, community support officers (CSOs), neighbourhood and street wardens, other forms of municipal policing, private security guards and citizen volunteers.
- This mixed economy has developed in an uneven and ad hoc manner and relations between plural policing providers vary considerably from effective co-production through partnerships to mutual indifference and rivalry. All too often, relations are poorly organised and coordinated, suffer duplication of effort and are marked by competition and mistrust. Community intelligence about crime and anti-social behaviour is often ill-managed and underused.
- The blurred roles, responsibilities, powers and identities of, and between, plural policing personnel engender public confusion and create uncertainties over what can legitimately be expected of officers.
- Where coordination is well-organised through effective partnerships, there are significant benefits to community safety, crime prevention and public reassurance. Where the division of labour is well-coordinated, this facilitates effective information exchange, mutual understanding, respect and trust.

- Locally dedicated, visible patrol personnel that engage and work with communities can provide people with a stake in their own security, foster social cohesion and help regenerate areas. Geographically based, integrated teams that draw together different plural policing personnel can afford considerable community safety advantages and provide operational coordination.
- Close cooperative relations between plural policing providers can encourage innovative styles of delivering security and order, a 'cross fertilisation' of good practice and greater awareness and responsibility for crime on the part of businesses, groups and individuals.
- Focusing on visible security solutions to the problem of disorder and anti-social behaviour alone can heighten anxieties, foster exclusionary tendencies and reinforce inter-group differences.
- There is an urgent need to consolidate and clarify relations between members of the 'extended policing family' and secure suitably robust forms of governance and regulation to ensure policing is delivered in accordance with democratic values of justice, equity, accountability and effectiveness.

The study found considerable evidence of public frustration with traditional levels of 'public' policing and apparent inadequacies of police responses to calls, particularly in residential sites. This perceived lack of sufficient or appropriate police response was identified by many citizens, local politicians and business people as the primary driving force in creating a market for additional security and policing services.

The current state of the mixed economy in policing through visible patrols in England and Wales has become highly competitive as different providers of policing vie against each other to access finite public and private resources. This has become particularly evident with the widespread entry of police into the security marketplace.

The research highlights the following key functions of visible security personnel:

- patrol and visibility;
- crime prevention and problem solving;
- environmental management and improvement;
- community engagement;
- linking and referral;
- information and intelligence gathering; and
- law enforcement.

Striking an appropriate balance between these (potentially competing) functions is central to the success of visible policing personnel depending on their ultimate aims and priorities.

The research highlights the importance of building inter-organisational trust and effective communication in the deployment of patrol personnel. Clear and consistent communication of the role, aims and limitations of specific personnel can help build effective inter-agency working relations.

Providing patrol personnel with additional powers to issue fixed penalty notices, as with CSOs or through accreditation schemes, may transform the nature of their role and public interactions. Enhancing their powers is likely to draw patrol officers into more adversarial relations, potentially placing them in more dangerous situations. The exercise of legal powers also raises questions concerning individual human rights, and requires robust procedures for ensuring that powers are appropriately used.

The research highlights the importance of engaging with residents and businesses, exploiting their knowledge about local crime and disorder problems and providing them with a stake in their own civic governance. Good community consultation at both strategic and operational levels was identified as important in establishing and maintaining community engagement and helping to build constructive and informed relationships.

The research also highlights significant evidence of a 'cross-fertilisation' effect where plural policing bodies work in close partnerships, especially where this occurs at an operational level. Close cooperation encourages:

- innovative styles of policing and reflective cultural sensibilities with regard to the delivery of security and order;
- greater awareness and responsibility for crime on the part of businesses, groups and individuals;
- informal management of incidents by private security and municipal personnel before requiring police intervention;
- the adoption of wider 'quasi-public' functions by security personnel;
- greater emphasis on proactive crime prevention and loss minimisation in the police; and
- a more significant role for the police as the repository of crime-related data and as information advisers and facilitators in collective local security-related endeavours.

The short-term nature of many contracts for additional policing and of government funding initiatives engenders a piecemeal approach to the mixed economy. This generates significant turnover and flux in the delivery of community safety. Furthermore, it often serves to undermine the development of strong bonds between policing personnel and local communities as funding shifts, providers are replaced and the priorities of initiatives change.

Coordination is best ensured if it is delivered at a number of mutually reinforcing and supportive levels:

- joined-up national initiatives and policies;
- regional oversight;
- strategic coordination and partnership;
- operational and front-line coordination.

Government needs to reflect on whether new initiatives and policies encourage conditions that will foster and sustain joint partnerships and collaborative local action. Many providers of plural policing do not have organisational boundaries coterminous with police forces. Hence, regional oversight could provide important cross-force coordination and standards setting and promote best practice.

Crime and disorder reduction partnerships (CDRPs) are an important vehicle in assisting coordination and providing a degree of local oversight. To do so, these partnerships, which remain dominated by the public sector, need to engage more actively with commercial policing providers and the private sector more generally.

Central to the delivery of operational coordination is the dedication of patrol personnel to specific geographic areas or sectors. Where possible, these should be localised to small areas so that individual officers can build up trust with their local communities and visitors. Coterminous boundaries of different plural policing personnel and organisations will facilitate coordination. Geographically based, integrated teams that draw together personnel from different policing organisations can afford:

- a clearer division of labour and organisation of respective roles and responsibilities of partners, reducing duplication and conflict;
- better understanding of the limitations of different partner organisations and personnel;
- clearer mutual expectations for different visible patrol personnel and provider organisations;
- enhanced and stable inter-personal and inter-organisational relations of trust and confidence;
- improved data exchange between the parties.

Different models for delivering operational coordination include:

- Linked policing teams, where plural policing personnel work alongside each other within dedicated geographic areas, liaising with regard to information exchange but not the subject of joint tasking or integrated supervision and management.
- Police-organised integrated police teams that incorporate police officers and police staff dedicated to specific local policing areas under the supervision and control of a police manager.

- Police-organised extended policing teams that include policing personnel beyond the 'immediate police family', such as street or neighbourhood wardens, parks police or other security and environment officers, dedicated to specific local policing areas under the supervision and control of a police manager.
- Local authority-organised extended policing teams, where plural policing personnel are integrated into teams managed by council officers outside of police employment.

Confident and effective information exchange is central to policing partnerships. Information exchange relies on, and also reinforces, positive relations between partners and mutual trust. The effectiveness of information exchange arrangements is a reflection of the effectiveness of the partnership as a whole. Concerns over confidentiality and data protection often thwart close partnership cooperation. Police sometimes invoke data protection regulations as a reason for non-engagement with partnership working. Some concerns are often based on poor understanding of the data protection regime and the powers to disclose information under the 1998 Crime and Disorder Act.

The research suggests that the rigorous collation, analysis and use of community intelligence gathered by patrol personnel remains the exception rather than the norm. In part, this is due to the large volume and the low-level nature of much intelligence, but is also a product of the significant cultural and organisational obstacles surrounding police information gathering, analysis and exchange and the institutionalisation of intelligence-led policing. In particular, information generated by neighbourhood wardens and private security patrols is often poorly used by the police. The collection, analysis and dissemination of information tend to be ad hoc and informal. There is often little linkage between community intelligence, reassurance activities and National Intelligence Model integration. Nevertheless, local information gathered by non-police patrol personnel, particularly where they benefit from acute local knowledge, can be of significant use in community policing and crime prevention endeavours.

Given the uneven coordination, weak accountability and segmented regulation of policing, this report calls on government to review the current workings of the diverse mechanisms for regulating security patrols, with a view to joining up the various forms of governance. It proposes establishing new regional policing boards to ensure appropriate standards, promote effective joint working and safeguard the public interest. Establishing regional policing boards could provide independent oversight, ensure cross-force regulation and connect with the concentration of political resources within regional government.

The research highlights the need to secure suitably robust forms of accountability and regulation to ensure that policing is delivered in accordance with the democratic values of justice, equity and effectiveness. This can best be achieved operationally through integrated policing teams, strategically through local crime and disorder reduction partnerships and more broadly through proposed regional policing boards with responsibility for coordinating service delivery and providing oversight.

Key recommendations

- Government should consider ways to clarify the division of labour and address the blurring of roles across different forms of plural policing. It should review the current workings of the segmented mechanisms for regulating plural policing, with a view to joining up the various forms of governance. More fundamentally, it needs to reflect on whether new policy initiatives encourage conditions that foster and sustain joint partnerships and collaborative local action.
- Consideration should be given to establishing regional policing boards with responsibility for regulating and coordinating service delivery across plural policing providers. Regional policing boards could also provide a degree of democratic accountability where regional assemblies exist.
- Local CDRPs should be encouraged to engage more fully with the private sector and assist in the task of coordinating local policing services, providing local oversight of the 'extended policing family' and strengthening local accountability.
- Private security firms need to engage constructively with the new regulatory regime and the Security Industry Authority's (SIA) implementation. If the security sector is to become a significant partner in community safety, it needs to grasp the opportunity presented by regulation to drive up standards, improve practice and secure greater public confidence. The SIA's capacity to deliver robust regulation will be vital for establishing an industry that can be trusted by the police, other security providers and the public.
- Consideration should be given to greater public awareness and standardisation of uniforms for CSOs and clearer badging for accredited private security officers and wardens, to address problems of public confusion and uncertainty over what can legitimately be expected of specific personnel.
- The work of CSOs, their place within the police and their contribution to community safety need clarification and evaluation before significant or rapid expansion. Otherwise, CSOs are likely to suffer 'mission creep' and be drawn into diverse roles that may undermine their reassurance value.
- The policy of giving patrol personnel increased fixed penalty notice powers needs to be reviewed in the light of possible adverse impacts this may have on the central tasks of each type of officer.
- Police forces should consider institutional ways in which they can better engage with the 'extended policing family' and integrate civilian staff.
- Police forces need to develop more systematic and structured approaches to the collection, storage and use of community intelligence.
- Clearer career paths within and between police officers and civilian staff, warden schemes and private security should be mapped out, allowing for different points of entry and transfer of skills.

- In the light of recent case law, government should consider reviewing whether property law rights of landowners to exclude people without any test for reasonableness are appropriate in the context of modern 'quasi-public' spaces such as shopping malls and leisure centres.

Introduction

We live in an age in which global insecurities and risks mix with and inform more localised anxieties about incivilities and anti-social behaviour. Modern police forces must respond simultaneously to international threats to order in the form of terrorism and organised crime as well as serious crime and the large volume of low-level crime that blights local communities. However, modern pressures on the police have served to pull officers away from locally tied patrols into reactive duties. Meanwhile, public demands on police time have grown significantly, leaving little time for non-incident-based interaction between police and local communities. As demand has grown, so the effectiveness of the police response has diminished due to the congested burdens on it.

Reactive demands on the police have relegated the provision of crime prevention and patrol officers working in dedicated localities to a residual role. Despite the original Peelian vision of crime prevention as a central element of police work, the history of the professional police has been one in which, until recently, crime prevention has been defined in increasingly narrow and specialist terms and has been pushed to the margins of the police organisation. By contrast, the 'rebirth of private policing' (Johnston, 1993) has had crime and risk prevention at its very heart.

Despite various attempts to promote community or neighbourhood policing over the past two decades, the reactive, crime-fighting focus of the police has served to undermine this, fuelled by internal organisational reforms and an emphasis on quantitative performance management. Government and organisational pressures to measure and monitor performance, in the name of efficiency, have caused the police to prioritise quantifiable activities. In a management culture in which 'what gets measured gets done', public reassurance through locally responsive patrols has lost out. This has served to reduce the public's sense of ownership over, or investment in, formal professional policing, impacting adversely on public confidence in the police.

> There has been a tendency, for sound reasons, and my Force is as guilty as any, of concentrating on those things that are going to impact on performance targets and, quite frankly, having somebody walk around a village or a housing estate is not necessarily going to directly impact on those performance targets. So we've stopped doing it in a large measure. (Chief Constable, interview)

Developments over the past 20 years or so have clouded the importance of the police's role as peacekeepers and of policing activities that win the trust of local people by engaging with them. Recent research found that the police had become "less responsive, less visible, less accessible and less engaged with the community" than the public would like (Fitzgerald et al, 2002, p xxi).

A reassurance paradox

We faced something of a reassurance paradox: as general crime risks have declined, so perceptions of victimisation risks have increased. Since 1995, both the British Crime Survey (BCS) and recorded police figures have shown a turnaround in the historic long rise of crime, which has dominated public debate. According to the BCS, the overall crime rate fell by 35.8% between 1995 and 2003 (Simmons and Dodd, 2003). Findings from the BCS 2003/04 demonstrated an overall fall in crime of 5% on the previous year. Despite this reduction, 48% of the public still thought that crime in their area had increased and 65% thought that crime across the country had increased over the previous two years. Figure 1 shows that despite falling crime rates there is a strong perception that crime is in fact increasing. The perception is both significant and enduring.

Figure 2 shows that public concerns have appeared to be largely unaffected by reductions in crime risks. More specifically, concerns over low-level incivilities and anti-social behaviour have continued to increase.

Figure 1: Beliefs about changes in the national crime rate (1996-2003/04) BCS

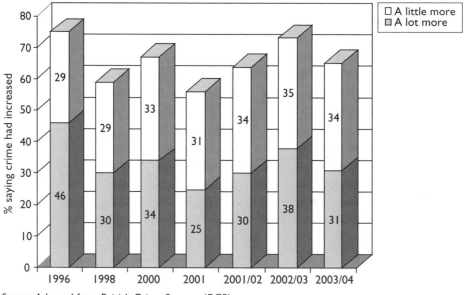

Source: Adapted from British Crime Surveys (BCS)

Figure 2: BCS trends in crime, fear and incivilities

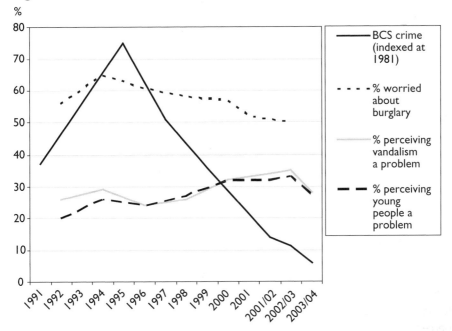

Source: BCS (adapted from Innes, 2004)

Consequently, the public has increasingly lost confidence in the capacity of the professional police, notably to deliver locally based visible patrols (Mirrlees-Black, 2001). Of particular concern is the finding that the more contact the public has with the police, the more their confidence in the service declines, unlike other public services such as schools and hospitals. Research also highlights that public confidence in the police is the strongest predictor of overall confidence in how well crime is dealt with at a local level. When asked directly what it would take to convince the public that crime was being dealt with more effectively, 'an increased police presence' was the most frequent answer (27%) (Page et al, 2004). Paradoxically, then, with police officer numbers at an all-time high and more civilian staff than ever before, as well as declining aggregate crime rates, public insecurity and fear of crime remain stubbornly high.

Government and police managers now acknowledge that public anxieties can no longer be discounted as irrational, but need to be responded to and addressed. If 'seeing is believing', as the Home Secretary recognised in a speech in March 2004 at the launch of the recent 'reassurance programme', it is now felt that the public needs to see a difference in the level of visible patrols to feel reassured. In today's 'citizen-focused policing', giving the public what they want in the form of visible patrol officers has become a major challenge for the police and government.

However, the police are not alone in responding to this public demand. To some considerable degree, the police are relative latecomers to this acknowledgement, as other providers have filled the perceived vacuum left by the withdrawal of dedicated police personnel and raised expectations over security. We now have an evolving mixed economy of uniformed patrols in which the private sector has considerably expanded both in numbers and in the range of operations (Jones and Newburn, 1998). Visitors to shopping malls, city centre arcades, airports and sports stadia, as well as night-clubs and bars around the country are as likely to come into contact and interact with non-police visible security personnel as they are with police constables.

Against a background of apparently growing anxieties about crime and anti-social behaviour and the decline in figures of authority, businesses, retail groups, housing associations, local authorities and property developers are increasingly purchasing supplementary forms of security, including visible patrol personnel. There is a recognition that the provision of local policing and security no longer resides solely with the police but has become increasingly fragmented and multi-tiered.

Plural policing

In this study, we make reference to the concept 'plural policing' in preference to other terms currently in vogue, such as 'public–private policing' and 'the extended police family'. We use this term for the following reasons:

- it recognises the plurality of policing providers and personnel and acknowledges the existence of a mixed economy;
- it breaks free from an unhelpful dichotomy between 'public' and 'private' police – recognising that the public police sometimes serve private and parochial interests and police private spaces, while private security is often funded by public authorities and operates in public spaces or privately owned spaces that have taken on a decidedly public character;
- it does not prioritise either implicitly or explicitly the role of any particular provider. Nor does it assume the nature of the relations between providers, unlike the rather misleading concept of the 'extended police family'.

For our purposes 'policing' is defined as intentional action involving the conscious exercise of power or authority (by an individual or organisation) that is directed towards rule enforcement, the promotion of order or assurances of safety. However, our focus is primarily on visible patrol, crime prevention and reassurance activities, rather than the array of other roles and functions performed by policing and security agents, notably in relation to crime detection and investigation.

The research study

This research draws on a two-year study of the developing mixed economy in forms of visible patrols and the shifting nature of the division of labour therein.

Aims

The research aims to provide an overview of significant developments in the provision of reassurance policing within England and Wales and to analyse the dynamic relations between different policing providers. More specifically, it aims to:

- map out the extent and range of plural policing activities and developments existing in England and Wales;
- explain the capacity and limitations that different providers have in meeting the divergent needs of different purchasers and beneficiaries in different contexts;
- compare and contrast the different styles of policing produced by and within the various configurations of plural policing;
- highlight implementation lessons learnt from innovative policing partnerships;
- consider institutional means for coordinating and harnessing plural policing arrangements and networks to contribute to the 'public good'; and
- produce policy-relevant recommendations, particularly with regard to the possible regulation of plural policing.

Working methods

The study combined two distinct datasets reflecting both a macro- and micro-level analysis of national developments and a series of six focused case studies. Much of the recent research has merely provided snapshots of focused evaluations regarding the effectiveness of particular patrol personnel (within specific contexts), without locating these within the broader complex of relations between diverse auspices and providers or the sum of collective endeavours. Given the rapid pace of change and waves of policy programmes, a two-year study allowed a broader temporal consideration of the relevance and impact of various initiatives. The in-depth local studies provided a thick description of micro-level interactions over a sustained period of time, affording specific and comparative insights to inform national developments.

National developments were analysed on the basis of interviews with key stakeholders from different organisations involved in the delivery and regulation of plural policing and a national survey of private security firms. This was supported by meetings and insights provided by an Advisory Board of key national contributors to policy debates, practice developments and research findings (see Appendix B for Advisory Board membership).

Six focused case studies were selected according to a number of criteria: (a) the existence of a vibrant mixed economy of diverse forms of visible patrol personnel and providers; (b) a degree of media or professional acclaim regarding the successful implementation of community safety partnerships; (c) an attempt to reflect different kinds of locations in which plural policing occurs, namely residential, commercial and industrial areas; and (d) the intention collectively to incorporate all the key forms of plural policing currently operating in England and Wales.

The case studies include the following (see Appendix A for more details):

- *Bradford City Centre*, a city centre police division combining local police, community support officers, private security guards and street wardens.
- *Liverpool Gold Zones*, a major city centre, combining contracted police constables, street crime wardens, private security guards, 'navigator' wardens and local police.
- *MetroCentre, Gateshead*, Britain's largest out-of-town shopping complex, combining contracted police officers, centre-managed private security guards and in-store security.
- *Trafford Park Industrial Estate, Greater Manchester*, Britain's largest industrial estate, combining dedicated police constables, private security guards and neighbourhood wardens.
- *Halton Moor Estate, Leeds*, a relatively high-crime residential area, combining neighbourhood wardens, private security patrols and local police.
- *Foxwood Estate, York*, a relatively low-crime residential area, combining private security patrols and local police.

In each of these case study areas, the research draws on diverse qualitative and quantitative data, including surveys of local people, businesses and patrol officers, focus group interviews with local residents and visitors, recorded crime and anti-social behaviour data and interviews with key practitioners involved in the delivery and coordination of plural policing endeavours.

A mixed economy of plural policing

2

National policy developments

We now have what government refers to as an 'extended police family', in which police officers have been joined by a diversity of community support officers, neighbourhood and street wardens, municipal rangers, private security guards and vigilant citizens. In this context, reassurance policing is increasingly becoming 'additional', provided and authorised by a plurality of policing personnel and auspices. In recent years, a number of important policy and legislative developments have shaped the current mixed economy of patrolling and visible policing.

The marketisation of police services

While the 1964 Police Act had allowed police forces to charge for 'special services', such as the policing of football matches, the 1994 Police and Magistrates Court Act allows the police to charge more widely for goods and services, including the contracting out of police officer time. Increasingly, police forces have sought to exploit this freedom to generate income externally, albeit that the growth of contracting has been uneven across forces in England and Wales, in large part dependent on local opportunities and the attitudes of senior officers.

1998 Crime and Disorder Act

The 1998 Act places a statutory duty on local authorities and the police together to develop, coordinate and promote crime and disorder reduction partnerships (CDRPs). The local police authority, probation service and health authority all have a statutory duty to participate in, and cooperate with, arrangements to develop a community safety strategy in the light of community consultation. From April 2003, police authorities and fire authorities became legally 'responsible authorities' for the purpose of formulating and implementing crime and disorder reduction strategies, as did Primary Care Trusts in April 2004. Section 17 of the 1998 Act requires local authorities, police authorities and national parks authorities to consider the crime and disorder implications of all their activities and decisions (the 2002 Police Reform Act added fire authorities to the list of organisations covered by section 17). Section 115 of the Act provides for the lawful disclosure of information between the 'responsible authorities' where necessary or expedient for the purposes of any provision of the Act. The Act also introduced the Anti-Social Behaviour Order.

Neighbourhood wardens programme

In 2000, the government launched a programme funding warden schemes to offer a semi-official presence in residential areas to improve quality of life and the local environment. Warden schemes have been closely tied to an agenda of neighbourhood renewal advanced by the Social Exclusion Unit (SEU, 1998, 2001) and to government's commitment to revive public spaces (ODPM, 2002). The programme helped establish warden schemes across the country through funding, guidance and advice. Numerous schemes were established and are now operating, independently of government funding (ODPM, 2004).

Licensing of the private security industry

The 2001 Private Security Industry Act introduced the first national licensing regime for private security officers and their managers. The Act establishes the Security Industry Authority (SIA), launched in April 2003, to license and regulate all 'contract' private security providers. Licences will be granted only after a full criminal record check has been issued and suitable training undertaken. Licensing of door supervisors began in March 2004 and vehicle immobilisers (commonly known as 'clampers') commence at the end of 2004. Manned guarding will be licensed during 2005.

Expanded use of fixed penalty notices for disorder and anti-social behaviour

The 2001 Criminal Justice and Police Act authorises the use of fixed penalty notices by police for a range of disorder and anti-social behaviour offences. The 2003 Anti-Social Behaviour Act extends fixed penalty powers to community support officers (CSOs), local authority officers and accredited persons. It also enables penalty notices for disorder for 16- to 17-year-olds.

Police reform agenda: phase one

The 2002 Police Reform Act introduced a first wave of reforms, including the new civilian role of CSOs. Without the full powers or training of a sworn police officer, CSOs seek to provide public reassurance by being dedicated to patrol and can issue fixed penalty notices. CSOs in six pilot areas were given powers to detain for up to 30 minutes pending the arrival of a police constable. The first CSOs started work on the streets of London in September 2002. The government committed to expand the number of CSOs to 4,000 by 2005. The Act also enables chief police officers to establish and maintain schemes that accredit suitably skilled and trained non-police employees to undertake specified support functions and issue penalty notices for disorder. Accredited community safety officers may be local authority, housing association or private security employees.

Police Standards Unit

The Police Standards Unit was set up by the Home Secretary in July 2001 as part of the government's police reform agenda. The focus of the unit's activities is to measure and compare basic command unit and local CDRP performance, understand the underlying causes of performance variations and identify and disseminate good practice.

Policing Bureaucracy Taskforce

This taskforce was established in 2002 under the guidance of Sir David O'Dowd, former Chief Inspector of Constabulary, as part of the government's police reform programme to seek ways to increase the presence of uniformed officers in the community by removing unnecessary burdens borne by front-line staff, providing adequate support and revising working practices. This has included identifying a package of ancillary tasks where responsibility for their delivery could be passed from the police to local authorities and encouraging income-generation activities within the police. In 2004, the government announced that by cutting bureaucracy and improving scientific and technical support it will free up the equivalent of 12,000 police officers for front-line duties by 2008.

Anti-Social Behaviour Action Plan

In October 2003, the government published an Anti-Social Behaviour Action Plan providing the basis for a national campaign against anti-social behaviour that 'puts the needs of the community first' by improving local responses across the country. It identified a number of action areas, including tackling nuisance neighbours, begging and environmental crime, while supporting victims and witnesses.

2003 Anti-Social Behaviour Act

The 2003 Act extends powers to CSOs, local authority officers and accredited persons to issue fixed penalty notices (provided by the 2001 Criminal Justice and Police Act) with regard to anti-social behaviour. It also enables fixed penalty notices for disorder to be issued to 16- to 17-year-olds. The Act creates a new power to disperse groups of two or more people from previously designated areas where there is believed to be persistent anti-social behaviour and a problem with groups causing intimidation. Police officers and CSOs will have a discretionary power to disperse groups for up to 24 hours, where their presence or behaviour has resulted, or is likely to result, in a member of the public being harassed, intimidated, alarmed or distressed.

Reassurance policing programme

The influential Her Majesty's Inspectorate of Constabulary (HMIC) thematic inspection report *Open all hours* highlighted police 'visibility, accessibility and familiarity' as three essential components of reassurance (Povey, 2001). The concept of reassurance was described as the 'primary objective' for policing in the National Policing Plan 2003-06. This message has been continued in the recently published plan (2004-07), which makes provision of a 'citizen-focused' service a key priority. Launched in March 2004, the reassurance policing programme aims to strengthen community involvement in policing to identify and tackle crimes that fuel fear in local neighbourhoods. The Police Standards Unit is providing more than £5 million over two years to trial the programme in 16 sites across eight police forces in England. The programme is aimed at delivering dedicated high-visibility police, making officers more accessible to local residents and increasing the quality and quantity of community intelligence. It aims to target the 'things that matter most' to local people and acknowledges that despite falling crime, policing should seek to address subjective public fears and falling confidence.

2004 Spending Review

In July 2004, the government announced its intention to increase the number of CSOs by a further 20,000 by March 2008, over and above the 4,000 target identified in the first national policing plan. This expansion is to be funded through a new Neighbourhood Policing Fund. At the same time, the government announced the continued funding of wardens through the Neighbourhood Renewal Fund, with a budget each year of £525 million until 2008.

Police reform agenda: phase two

In November 2003, the government published a Green Paper, *Policing: Building safer communities together* (Home Office, 2003), outlining a second wave of reform. Building on this, and the consultation process to which it gave rise, a White Paper, *Policing: Modernising police powers to meet community needs* (Home Office, 2004c), was published in August 2004. Proposals include significantly extending CSOs' role by giving them powers to issue warnings to beggars, confiscate alcohol from underage drinkers, enforce local by-laws, direct traffic and search some suspects for weapons. In November 2004, a further White Paper was published, entitled *Building communities, beating crime* (Home Office, 2004d), setting out plans to support the development of dedicated neighbourhood policing teams across the country, introduce a national non-emergency telephone number and put in place (by the end of 2006) guaranteed standards of customer service to the public whenever they have contact with the police, thus creating a policing 'contract'. Police forces across the country are to be empowered to give CSOs the power of detention. The White Paper also initiated a review of the role, work and accountability of CDRPs established by the 1998 Crime and Disorder Act. The review will result in a White Paper on community safety to be published in 2005.

Police workforce strength

As Figure 3 illustrates, overall police workforce numbers have increased over the past decade, albeit this period also witnessed a decline in the number of special constables and traffic wardens. In 2002, there was a ratio of 8.8 specials to 100 police officers, compared with 13.1 per 100 police officers 15 years earlier and 62.8 per 100 officers in 1961. The continuing fall in the number of traffic wardens in part reflects the increasing transfer of responsibilities to local authorities for traffic control.

Figure 3: Police numbers in England and Wales (31 March 1993-31 March 2004)

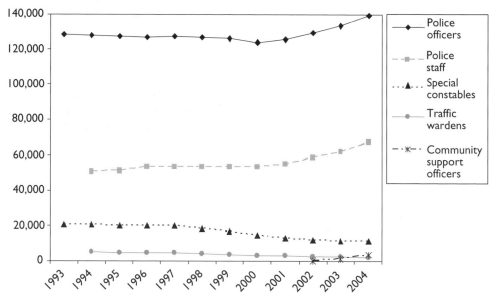

Source: Christopherson and Cotton (2004, p 13)

Figure 4: Police service strength by type of employee as at 31 March 2004

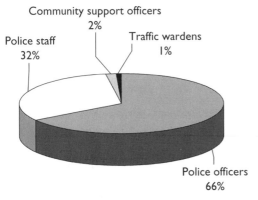

Community support officers
2%

Traffic wardens
1%

Police staff
32%

Police officers
66%

Source: Christopherson and Cotton (2004, p 2)

Latest figures show there were 139,200 police officers in England and Wales at the end of March 2004. This takes the total number of the immediate police family to 214,365, including 67,597 police staff, 3,417 CSOs and 1,652 traffic wardens. More than a third of police employees are not sworn constables (see Figure 4). In addition, there are 10,988 special constables. Police employees are supplemented by more than 1,500 street or neighbourhood wardens in some 200 schemes across the country funded through the Neighbourhood Wardens Team in the Office of the Deputy Prime Minister. In addition, there are estimated to be a further 2,000 other wardens funded through different sources.

Government's commitment to expand significantly the number of CSOs in England and Wales will radically reshape the face of frontline policing, transforming the current ratio of CSOs to police officers from approximately one in 35 to almost one in six by 2008 (see Figure 5).

Figure 5: Projected police service strength by type of employee for 2008

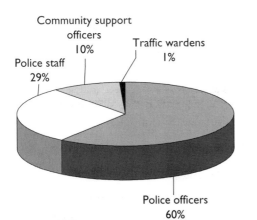

Community support officers
10%

Traffic wardens
1%

Police staff
29%

Police officers
60%

CSOs have become the linchpin in convincing the public that the government is taking crime and the fear of crime seriously and responding to public demands for more uniformed officers on the streets. For the government, increasing police visibility through CSO deployment is a key means of realising tangible public sector reform that impacts on front-line service delivery, something that critics say it has been slow (or unable) to achieve.

Commercial developments

It is estimated that between 300,000 and 500,000 people are employed in the private security industry. Not all of these personnel are visible security guards. As well as contracted security guards, there are many 'in-house' employees with primary or secondary security functions. According to the British Security Industry Association (BSIA, 2001), there are an estimated 2,000 manned security companies and over 125,000 dedicated security officers[1]. The estimated turnover of the manned security sector in 2003 was more than £1.8 billion, nearly a threefold increase on the figure 10 years earlier and some 14 times greater than the total 20 years previously (Figure 6).

Figure 6: BSIA members turnover by sector (£ million)

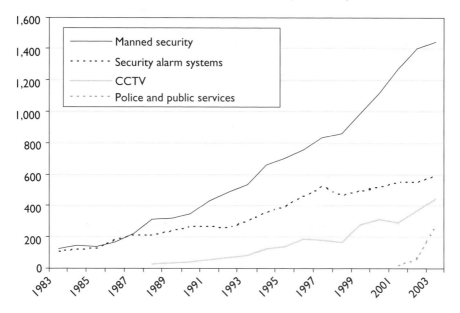

Source: BSIA. The turnover of BSIA member companies is based on their annual declarations. The number of member companies supplying statistics has risen from 63 in 1981 to 515 at the end of 2003

---

[1] The manned security sector is that part of the private security industry that employs security officers to protect people and property in a wide variety of environments.

The BSIA estimates that, at the end of 2003, its members' share of the manned security market was 79% and the total industry turnover (including non-members) stood at £1,883 million. By contrast, the BSIA share of the CCTV market was estimated to be 88%, meaning that the total industry turnover was approximately £509 million. The BSIA established its Police and Public Services Section in 2001 for companies that provide support services to the police and related public sector organisations. By the end of 2003, the estimated share of this sector was 92%, making an industry total turnover of £290 million[2].

Figure 7 shows the dramatic growth in the number of people employed within the manned security sector during the 1990s. Since 2001, this growth has stabilised; in part this might be a consequence of the anticipated introduction of licensing. Nevertheless, the growth in the police and public services sector reflects important shifts within the industry.

While the size and spread of private security grew significantly in the second half of the twentieth century and the total police workforce increased, Britain has also witnessed a dramatic decline in the number of 'secondary social control'

Figure 7: BSIA members number of employees by sector

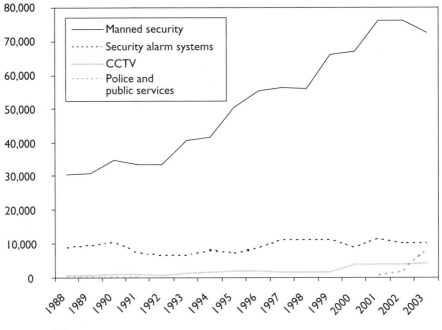

Source: BSIA

---

[2] With some 81 members in 2004, the Police and Public Services section was established for companies that provide support services to the police and related public sector organisations. It focuses on providing improved standards and tailored training for the activities involved, recognising the difference that such public functions entail.

Table 1: Primary and secondary social control occupations in Britain

	1951	1971	1991
Police officers	84,585	115,170	149,964
Security guards and related	66,950	129,670	159,704
'Roundsmen/roundswomen'	98,143	48,360	49,182
Bus (and tram) conductors	96,558	57,550	2,471
Train ticket inspectors/guards	35,715	46,800	15,642

Note: Estimates from Census
Source: Jones and Newburn (2002, p 141)

occupations (Jones and Newburn, 2002). These occupations often had a visible (frequently uniformed) presence within communities and public places and performed a secondary security function and provided 'natural surveillance' alongside their primary roles as, for example, bus conductors, park keepers, caretakers, roundsmen/women (those delivering milk, newspapers, etc) and train guards (see Table 1). The decline of many of these occupations has removed a degree of latent security and natural surveillance from many communities.

Survey of manned private security firms

The establishment of the SIA signals the growing role of the private security industry within the mixed economy of policing. This research aimed to engage with the industry by seeking their views on recent developments and the organisation of the industry more generally. In this context, a national survey of manned private security companies was conducted in the summer of 2003[3].

The survey found that nearly half of companies (47%) said that public sector contracts constituted less than 10% of their manned security work. By contrast, more than a third (35%) said that this figure was between 10% and 30% and declared it to be over 30% of their total. A small number of firms were engaged in significant public sector contracting; 9% said that more than 60% of their work was with the public sector, representing firms of varying sizes.

More than one fifth (21%) identified residential areas as holding the greatest potential for growth, despite the fact that only a limited number had a significant involvement in this field, while only 2% identified residential areas as their most financially important sphere of work at the time of survey (see Figure 8).

---

[3] Completed questionnaires were received from 139 companies, 46 of which were BSIA members (a 45% response rate from BSIA members).

Figure 8: Potential growth areas over the next five years in the manned security sector

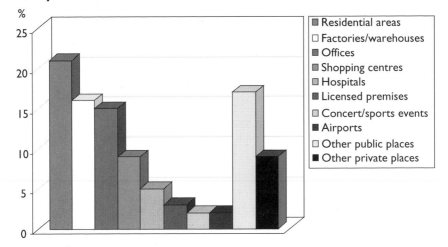

Some 63% strongly welcomed the introduction of the national licensing scheme established by the 2001 Private Security Industry Act and another 31% welcomed it. Unsurprisingly, the larger manned security firms were more likely to strongly welcome licensing. Respondents agreed that licensing would improve public perceptions of the private security industry (85%); reduce the number of criminals operating within the industry (80%); improve the general standards of service delivery (73%); and improve relations with the police (61%); as well as increase costs to the security industry (95%) and concentrate market activity across a smaller number of companies (79%).

> I am concerned that the tone of statements coming from the SIA, BSIA and others, plus the apparently heavy weighting of ex- and serving police officers on various committees and advisory groups could push the industry into becoming an adjunct of the police service. In my experience the police have always wanted to keep the manned guarding industry at a distance, now they seem to be having an inappropriate influence on it. (Survey respondent)

A majority of firms (52%) thought that licensing would increase pressures for organisations to purchase in-house security, currently unregulated by the SIA.

The majority (57%) felt it likely that they will apply to the local police for community safety accreditation of some or all of their security officers under the 2002 Police Reform Act. A third thought this very likely and nearly a quarter (24%) thought this likely. Most of the rest were uncertain (34% of the total), whereas 6% thought this unlikely and 4% very unlikely. When asked to explain their responses, those who had said they were likely to seek accreditation often did so because they believed it would improve relations with the police and/or increase business prospects and enhance their public status and credibility.

Respondents highlighted the importance of cooperation with the local police. Some 88% claimed cooperation with the local police to be important for their manned security operations (nearly two thirds of whom said it was very important).

While three fifths (61%) indicated that the level of cooperation with local police was good, a significant minority (39%) reported the level of cooperation to be not very good or poor. According to experiences of the companies, cooperation varied significantly between different police force areas. Some 59% said that cooperation was variable (of which 17% of the total said it was very variable).

> The difference between forces is huge. The cooperation level rests entirely on how useful our people are to the police, not the other way round. (Survey respondent)

Where the level of cooperation was good, a number of respondents noted the importance of interpersonal relations where private security managers had previously worked in the police. The following survey respondents highlight the importance of inter-organisational trust, against a background of distrust, in promoting the role of the private sector:

> The police in general and crime prevention officers in particular express concern at our expanding roles. Somehow the message must be delivered that the private security industry has a significant role to play.

> At the moment in time, it is a one-way street. This leads to mistrust and not full cooperation. The police in our area see all security operatives as the easier solution to achieving crime and disorder targets, despite training and qualifications of said operative. Not a true partnership. The legislation will build bridges.

> If the level of cooperation and trust was enhanced both the police and private security industry would benefit. The end result would be better crime prevention and a safer environment for the public to live in.

The survey revealed the following views on the future role of private security and the shape of relations with the police:

- Nearly three quarters of respondents agreed that the police should provide private security companies with greater access to crime data and security information.
- Just under half (45%) agreed that the extent to which the police are allowed to generate income by selling services should be restricted, as against 14% who disagreed.
- Forty-two per cent disagreed that the police should have a greater role in influencing the composition of local security markets. By contrast, a third agreed.
- Respondents were evenly split over whether private security officers should be given more legal powers. While 38% agreed, some 36% disagreed.

- A significant majority (88%) thought that the crime prevention role of security officers should continue to expand.
- Two fifths (39%) agreed (and only 14% disagreed) that the police reform agenda will intensify competition within the 'extended police family', despite its explicit intention to do otherwise.

The regulation of private security represents a significant challenge both to the regulatory authorities (SIA) and to the industry. Traditionally, the industry has been dominated by cost overriding service quality (despite the efforts of the BSIA). It has been an industry of low-skilled and poorly paid labour, little investment in career development and high staff turnover, as well as minimal training and weak supervision (Button, 2002). In some parts of the industry, there is an annual staff turnover of up to 150%, and in some sectors up to 25% of staff are on minimum wages. Understandably, there has been a conventional lack of trust between the police and large sections of the private security industry. Regulation affords an opportunity to establish a threshold of professionalism and operational probity, grounded in skills, competencies and minimum standards. The capacity of the SIA to set appropriate standards and enforce them effectively will determine the level of confidence in regulation and trust in the efficacy of private security.

> The jury's out on how strict the SIA can be. I haven't seen one company yet put in the dock or one employee put in the dock because they're trading without a licence. When I see the first one I shall then be satisfied. Everything says to me that yes, their intentions are good. Pragmatically, however, I know that the first place that will suffer when they have a budget crisis will be enforcement because it is the most discretional of their activities and so if they start to find financial difficulties it will be interesting to see whether they continue to invest heavily as they said. In enforcement, if the SIA fails from minute one, never mind day one, if it fails to enforce, then it could destroy the whole philosophy of regulation. (ACPO representative)

The perceived quality of regulation will undoubtedly colour future police willingness to engage with the private sector, as it will influence public acceptance. Given the current legislative exemption, there remain considerable concerns about the potential movement of disreputable providers to the 'in-house' security sector. It may be difficult for the SIA to make a sufficient case to government to include 'in-house' security guards within its regime (thus removing its exemption status) without evidence of corruption or criminality within the 'in-house' security sector.

Both the survey findings and case studies demonstrate that relations between private security and police are highly variable and often dependent on informal networks and acquaintances, notably where security managers previously worked in the police. In some instances, private security firms forge productive partnerships with police. In other instances, individual firms and guards have themselves been the focus of police concerns through their involvement in organised criminality.

For example, on the Trafford Park Industrial Estate, concerns about some of the activities of some private security guards and firms was a stimulus behind the introduction of a voluntary system of licensing and regulation (the Guardsafe scheme). There remains a view among some police that security firms are part of the problem, not the solution. While understandable in a limited number of cases, this view needs to be challenged if partnership agendas are to become institutionalised.

The current regulation of private security by the SIA presents a considerable opportunity to improve the professionalism, quality and standing of the industry and affords the prospect for police and local authorities to work with private security to provide effective policing that meets local needs. If the private security industry is to play a greater role in community safety, it needs to be fit for the 'public' tasks this entails. Community safety accreditation schemes offer a channel for the police and private security to engage in more productive relations and enhance cooperation.

A competitive marketplace in the mixed economy

There was considerable evidence from the case studies of public frustrations with the traditional level of normal public policing and the perceived inadequacies of police responses to calls, particularly in residential sites. This perceived lack of sufficient or appropriate police response was identified by many citizens, local politicians and business people as the primary driving force in creating a market for additional security and patrol services.

The current state of the mixed economy in policing through visible patrols in England and Wales has become highly competitive as different providers and forms of policing vie with each other to access finite public and private resources. This has become particularly evident with the widespread entry of the police into the patrol marketplace.

- The price of private security is set to rise with the introduction of national licensing and regulation by the SIA.
- It is estimated that some 30% of manned security guards may have to leave the industry and as a result of price inflation some of the market share may transfer to surveillance and security technology.
- The cost of police-employed patrol personnel has been reduced with the introduction of CSOs.
- The current and future funding of CSOs will become increasingly linked to income generation through subcontracting and matched funding arrangements.

The introduction of CSOs has significantly increased the competitive edge of the police within the additional security market. As dedicated patrol officers with limited powers, CSOs are freed from most of the pressures that serve to abstract constables from dedicated contractual arrangements that often stymie the commercial marketing of police (Crawford et al, 2003). Cost is crucial in a marketplace where the BSIA estimates that 60% of security contracts are awarded on price alone. CSOs are also able to retain a competitive advantage over their non-police rivals on the basis of the sacred and symbolic reassurance value of the police uniform and the emotional investment by the British public in their 'Bobbies', as well as the logistical and organisational support available to CSOs (Crawford et al, 2004).

However, for many local forces, recruiting CSOs has been as much a pragmatic desire to augment resources as a fundamental belief in their effectiveness, as the following Chief Constable recognised:

> There was a sense in which driving it forward was as much about the need to maximise resources from wherever as it was about any particular ideological position around, for example, what can you use a CSO for and what can't you use a CSO for? (Chief Constable)

As another Chief Constable frankly noted, CSOs enable the police to provide a cheaper form of visible policing:

> There's no question at all, they've been brought in as a cheaper method of delivering some elements of policing. By making them part of the police service you give chief constables the opportunity to employ cheaper resources but no one's admitted that because it upsets the apple cart. There's absolutely no doubt at all in my mind, and I welcome it absolutely. Police officers are very good at doing a particular range of jobs but you don't need all the skills which you've got in a police officer to do some of the things that CSOs do and, what is more, if you give CSOs a job to do, they'll do it a darned sight better than some police officers will because police officers very often want the exciting bits, the television image of being a police officer. CSOs want to do some of the things that police officers get bored with doing, but they are critical elements of delivering reassurance visibility to the community. So I think they are a simple political expediency of getting second-tier policing without calling it that. (Chief Constable)

Nevertheless, CSOs have given the police a renewed confidence in competing in the patrol marketplace and thereby 'regain the streets' from municipal and private policing rivals. Some police managers believe that CSOs can even undercut the cost of private security.

The nature of relations also prompts competition between different styles of policing, notably in the balance between enforcement, patrol, community cohesion, crime prevention and problem solving (to which we return in Chapter 3). Different policing styles may be in an antagonistic relationship with each other. They may reflect competing aims and methods and create differing demands on police time and resources. This underscores the importance of the division of labour within policing networks being appropriately organised and coordinated.

Factors influencing the uneven development of the mixed economy and relations between plural policing providers include:

• Detectable variations in the approach of senior police managers towards the delivery of patrol, engagement with the private security sector and work with neighbourhood wardens/local authority patrols as well as willingness to enter a market for their services.
• The uneven manner in which local authorities have responded to the rising climate of fear and insecurity and the requirements of partnership working contained within recent legislation.
• Variations in local responses towards central government funding regimes, which aim to 'pump-prime' and stimulate the growth of various forms of plural policing.
• The uneven geographical development and spread of the private security industry in different sectors. In some areas, private security is dominated by small-scale providers with rapid turnover. In other areas, larger and more established firms dominate.

Selling police patrol services

Having entered the marketplace for additional patrols only recently, many police forces are experimenting with income-generation arrangements and consequently learning the challenges that this entails. Recent guidance from the Association of Chief Police Officers (ACPO) on income generation and sponsorship by police forces acknowledges that:

> It is very important to understand and manage customer needs. This is currently recognised as an area of weakness within most UK police forces. (ACPO, 2004, p 45)

One of the central difficulties that 'consumer needs' present for the police in selling patrol services revolves around the issue of operational control resting with police managers (ultimately the Chief Constable). Legally, the police can only justify such income-generation initiatives if they are in line with determined local and national priorities and plans and enhance service delivery. Private or parochial interests that pay for police naturally want control over the contracted officers. Given that officers ultimately remain public resources, they need to retain the operational 'final say' on how they are deployed. In emergencies or to cover for other officers, Chief Constables will want to be able to draw on officers regardless of whether they are contracted to specific patrol duties or not.

This means that a contractor of additional police patrol may purchase a resource but not have the ultimate say over its deployment or its availability. For some initiatives, this can become a stumbling block to implementation, particularly where a dedicated officer is frequently drawn away from their contracted work into wider operational duties (Crawford et al, 2003).

> We always retain operational responsibility and the councillors will never have the authority to tell us which streets to walk down or who to target, etc. We will be given objectives. How we achieve this is up to us. (Police officer)

Precisely these concerns were voiced at the inception of the MetroCentre policing initiative. However, in practice, this did not prove to be a problem as the officers largely remained in situ and were not pulled away from their duties within the centre. The fact that the contracted officers were based in a localised police station within the MetroCentre undoubtedly helped to cocoon them from the wider pressures confronting the Northumbria Police service.

In practice, so long as the activities of the additional contract fall within general policing priorities and local delivery plans, general deployment duties can be agreed between the police and contractor in the form of a service-level agreement. Further, 'customers fears' can be allayed by contractual terms or protocols specifying – in as restrictive a manner as possible – the conditions under which a dedicated officer would be legitimately abstracted from an additional patrolling initiative into wider operational duties. Furthermore, the arrival of CSOs as dedicated patrol officers has introduced a commodity that the police can sell with fewer fears over abstractions.

Nevertheless, where contractors purchase a police officer or CSO, they need to realise that operational control remains with the police. From the police perspective, responding to understandable pressures from purchasers for greater ownership of the purchased resource should sharpen the provision of additional mechanisms of accounting for the service provided, such as activities data, performance measurements and incident reports, so that contractors are made aware of how their money is being spent. If police forces are to immerse themselves further in contracting out patrol services, they will need to respond positively to the demands of contractual accountability that such arrangements presuppose and foster.

3

Strategies and styles of policing

Core tasks

V isible patrol personnel perform a variety of tasks with different objectives. In the course of the research, different types of patrol personnel were surveyed in order to elicit a picture of the different core tasks and skills required of them in the course of their work[1]. Respondents were asked to select from a list up to three statements that best reflect their core tasks. The key findings are set out in Figure 9 in relation to community support officers (CSOs), wardens and private security respectively. Unsurprisingly, the most common responses for CSOs were public reassurance (69%), intelligence gathering (65%), mobile patrols (42%), prevention of anti-social and youth nuisance behaviour (38%) and general crime prevention (35%).

Figure 9: Core tasks of different patrol personnel compared (%)

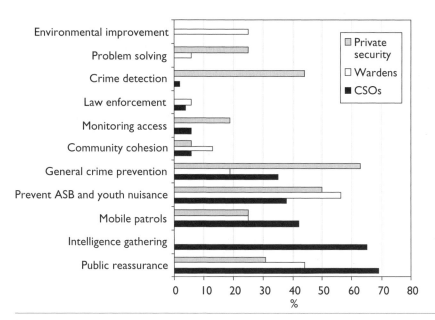

[1] The surveys were conducted in January and February 2004. For the sake of consistency the same survey was devised for all the different patrol officers. The CSO survey is based on 48 replies from the 76 CSOs working in West Yorkshire at the time (a response rate of 63%). The warden survey is based on replies from 16 street and neighbourhood wardens in Leeds. The private security survey is based on replies from 16 St James' security guards operating in the MetroCentre, Gateshead.

Figure 10: Most important skills of different patrol personnel compared (%)

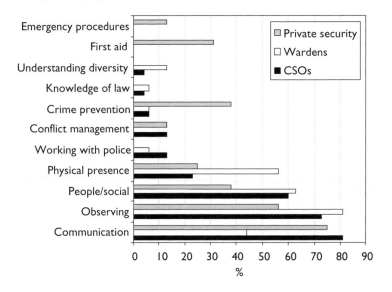

By contrast, the prevention of anti-social and youth nuisance behaviour (56%), public reassurance (44%), mobile patrols (25%) and environmental improvement (25%) were the most frequently cited core tasks of wardens. Private security guards highlighted general crime prevention (63%) and the prevention of anti-social and youth nuisance behaviour (50%), followed by crime detection (44%) and public reassurance (31%).

Skills

In the survey, patrol personnel were asked to identify the three most important skills they possess for the work they do. Figure 10 highlights the findings. It shows that for CSOs communication skills, observation and information gathering and people skills consistently were the three main responses.

When asked how well the training had prepared them for their work challenges, just over half of CSOs responded quite or very well (52%), but a significant percentage felt that it had not prepared them very well (40%) or not at all well (8%).

Functions

The research highlights the following key functions of visible security personnel:

- patrol function;
- crime prevention and problem-solving function;
- environmental management and improvement function;
- community engagement function;
- linking and referral function;
- information- and 'community intelligence'-gathering function; and
- law enforcement function.

Striking an appropriate balance between these functions is central to the success of visible policing personnel, depending on their ultimate aims.

Patrol

For some types of patrol personnel, notably CSOs and private security, their visible presence is primarily focused around deterrence and reassurance. For others, notably wardens, visibility is more concerned with building trust within and being accessible to residents within their communities.

Crime prevention and problem solving

There is significant scope to combine patrol with crime prevention and problem-solving activities. This requires patrol personnel to identify local problems and seek solutions to address the causes of those problems through prevention and partnerships with wider stakeholders. This may often require holistic interventions that involve residents or local people and solutions that extend beyond the narrow lens of crime control.

Crime prevention activities of CSOs in Bradford

CSOs conducted important crime prevention work, although scope remains for further development. In Bradford city centre where CSOs were first deployed, theft from a vehicle fell by 23% and theft of vehicle by 25%, while vehicle interference and tampering declined by 24%. Personal robbery declined by 46%. The greatest reductions occurred in crime 'hot-spot' areas, suggesting that patrol personnel were appropriately targeted through intelligence-led deployment. For many types of crime there does not appear to have been a significant displacement effect. However, some geographical displacement for certain types of crime, particularly theft from a vehicle, was apparent.

A contributing factor in the reduction of thefts from a vehicle in Bradford appears to have been linked to the crime prevention advice and activities of CSOs. For example, if CSOs see items of potential value on display in a parked vehicle, the registration details are recorded and a letter is sent to the owner warning them of the risk of this oversight. Alternatively, a warning leaflet is left on the windscreen to draw the vehicle owner's attention to their vulnerability.

CSOs in Bradford also conducted joint initiatives of truancy-related patrols in conjunction with the local education truancy officers and street wardens. CSOs record each incident where they identify young people truanting from school and details of the individuals are collected and passed to the local education authority. Between October and December 2003, CSOs in the city centre recorded some 125 such incidents. Arising from this, CSOs developed a template form so that information can be passed more efficiently to local authority truancy officers.

CSOs also distributed a large number of leaflets warning people about seasonal rises in mobile phone theft. Accordingly, information leaflets conveyed messages encouraging young people always to be vigilant when using mobile phones, as well as advice on reducing opportunities for thieves. CSOs worked closely with the student populations in Bradford, providing crime prevention advice. A surgery at the university was established to facilitate this work and to render CSOs more accessible to the student population.

These activities evidence the manner in which non-vehicle-based patrol enables police staff to pursue innovative forms of crime prevention. Indeed, officers on foot patrol are more likely to perceive opportunities to implement crime prevention strategies than those passing fleetingly by vehicle. Importantly, they also have more time to interact with the public and thus implement any devised strategies. While on patrol, therefore, CSOs might be encouraged to consider opportunities to introduce crime prevention strategies or dispense risk avoidance advice. It is in this context that further training for CSOs might include a greater element of crime prevention training.

Figure 11: Total number of recorded crimes on Halton Moor

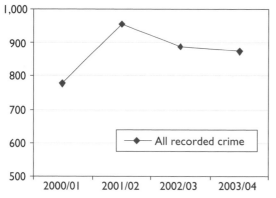

On the Halton Moor estate the total number of recorded crimes declined in each of the two years after the introduction of wardens in early 2002 (Figure 11). Having reached a peak in 2001-02, it declined by 7% in 2002-03 and by 1% in 2003-04, as compared with the year before. Notable reductions were to be found in burglaries (Figure 12) and thefts of and from vehicles. Although in the case of vehicle-related theft the relative volume of this crime is reasonably low in Halton Moor.

Figure 12: Burglary rate per 1,000 households (2000/04)

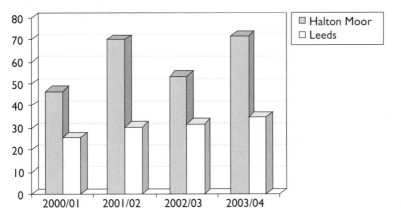

Robberies also saw a significant percentage decline, but the absolute number of such offences was small. By contrast, violent crime increased despite the presence of wardens, with nearly two and a half times as many violent offences recorded in the two years after April 2002 as compared with the previous two years. Levels of criminal damage fluctuated during the period (Figure 13). Some of the increase in the last year may have been due, in part, to the greater reporting by neighbourhood wardens.

Figure 13: Criminal damage rate per 1,000 population (2000/04)

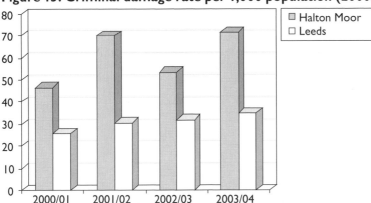

Environmental management and improvement

Given the link between 'grime and crime' and particularly the connection between the urban environment and people's fear of crime, patrol personnel can significantly assist in revitalising neighbourhoods and reconnecting people. As such, patrol personnel can help advance the government's 'liveability' agenda by contributing to 'cleaner, safer, greener' communities (ODPM, 2002). Improving the physical environment can be an important first step or corollary to improving community relations. Moreover, interventions into the physical environment can produce quick benefits for public reassurance, as urban areas are perceived as less threatening if they are kept clean and orderly. Environmental improvements may produce tangible and visible results and thus empower local people by convincing them that they can make a difference.

Wardens in particular have a significant environmental management function. This may be explicitly linked into the management of the council's housing stock, notably void properties, or more indirectly concerned with community regeneration. Within many neighbourhood warden schemes, for instance, the policing role is subordinate to the environmental or community cohesion functions.

Anti-social behaviour

Straddling crime prevention and environmental improvement is the growing concern for anti-social behaviour (ASB), which has attained a high political profile, promoted strongly by both local and national politicians. And yet, ASB is something of an ideological construct, lacking precise definition, transcending and connecting both criminal and subcriminal activities. It includes a range of problems such as noisy neighbours, abandoned cars, vandalism, graffiti, litter, youth nuisance and incivilities, but some of these are dependent on subjective interpretation and hence variable. There remain considerable difficulties in measuring ASB. The ASB One Day Count organised by the Home Office on 10 September 2003 attempted to do so, but this was a one-off event best suited to making inter-authority comparisons rather than arriving at a single value to represent 'the size of the ASB problem'.

Figure 14 highlights the number of ASB-related calls logged on the West Yorkshire Police command and control database in relation to Halton Moor over a two-year period from April 2002 to March 2004. The data show a series of peaks and troughs with no significant trend (either up or down) over time, nor are there any discernable seasonal variations.

Interpreting the data presented in Figure 14 with regard to the impact of wardens in the area is problematic, largely because two contradictory processes may be at play simultaneously. First, if wardens are having a positive effect, this may result in recorded incidents increasing as wardens report and log such incidents or

Figure 14: Recorded incidents of ASB on Halton Moor (April 2002-March 2004)

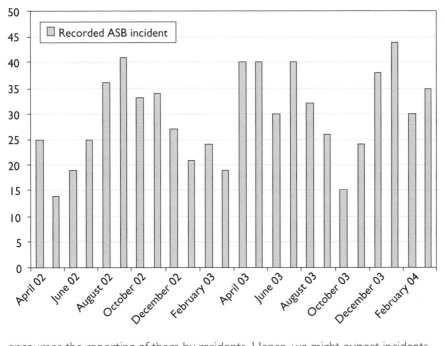

encourage the reporting of them by residents. Hence, we might expect incidents to rise over time. Second, if wardens are having a positive effect on the causes of ASB, through their work with young people for instance, we might expect levels to decline over time. The fluctuating levels in Halton Moor may be a product of both of these effects or neither of them, despite the fact that residents when surveyed in mid-2004 said that they believed crime and ASB had declined over the previous two years. Furthermore, given the relatively low number of incidents per month and the small geographic area covered, a certain degree of 'natural' or 'random' fluctuation is inevitable.

One particular manner in which the regulation of ASB has developed significantly in recent years has been with regard to the use of Anti-Social Behaviour Orders (ASBOs). In Leeds, the police, supported by the regional government office and council, opted to use high-media-profile, mass ASBOs. The most notable was the well-publicised operation 'Cape', in which ASBOs were issued against 66 young people in a small residential area of the city, Little London, on the same day in September 2003. As well as generating significant media attention, this approach of targeting reasonably serious persistent offenders (involved in crimes relating to public drug dealing) demonstrated to residents that the imaginative use of ASBOs could significantly impact on community safety. However, this 'big-bang' approach also generated certain logistical difficulties, notably with regard to legal issues and costs that largely fell on the council, provoking certain tensions.

The role of wardens in ASBOs has developed slowly. Where they have been involved, this has largely been concerned with information gathering and policing breaches. Anti-Social Behaviour Unit (ASBU) officers interviewed in Leeds saw this as an important and potentially growing role for wardens, particularly in cases where residents are unwilling to make statements against specific individuals because of fears of reprisals. Where successful, ASBOs are brought with the assistance of a warden against serious and persistent offenders who have had a detrimental impact on the local community; this can significantly enhance residents' views of wardens. Such work can be seen as tangible evidence that wardens can make a difference. However, it can also bring wardens into conflict with sections of a community and reinforce perceptions that they are an arm of law enforcement. Some wardens expressed concern about acting as professional witnesses. ASBU officers also commented that statements made by direct victims were preferable and made for stronger cases. As a consequence, wardens may prefer to work with victims to try to support and encourage them to make statements themselves.

By contrast, in Liverpool, both street wardens and navigators[2] were used as professional witnesses and concerns around community cohesion were less apparent. However, the navigators in particular were concerned about being seen as having a crime-fighting role in general as it conflicted with their other 'softer' roles.

The government's agenda for ASB affords an opportunity for wardens to work more closely with a wider array of local services beyond the police, housing departments and social landlords. Notably, wardens are beginning to work closer with environmental health officers (who have additional noise nuisance powers) and Trading Standards. In Leeds, relations with Trading Standards were improved through joint working around a city-wide Distraction Burglary project (Lister et al, 2004).

Linking and referral

Where they work well, front-line patrol personnel can play an important linking function connecting the diverse range of organisations that impact on community safety, both with each other and with members of the local community. Where CDRPs have sought to join up community safety provision at a strategic and middle-management level, front-line patrol personnel of different kinds can become the street-level links between local services; as such, they can address the 'institutional gaps' and 'coordination problems' that often exist. More specifically, patrol personnel can link together and enhance cooperation between the various plural policing providers.

---

[2] Navigators were council employed patrol personnel with an ambassadorial role working in Liverpool city centre.

Added to this, front-line patrol personnel have an important referral function moving people and information through and between appropriate organisations. They can help ensure that people do not 'fall between the gaps' and assist by referring them to relevant local services. To perform these functions, such personnel must have a good understanding of the local services and organisations available, their ways of working, capacities and limitations, as well as appropriate referral points. Given the relative absence of time pressures and the discretionary nature of their role, wardens are particularly well placed to work with vulnerable individuals within communities. However, the interaction that patrol personnel have with other service providers can mean that they become drawn into the ways in which these organisations work and, hence, may be seen by residents and others, erroneously or not, as closely associated with them. In the process, they may be perceived as losing a degree of independence, potentially an important element in community acceptance.

Given the discretionary nature of the warden's role, it is important that wardens are appropriately managed and sufficiently accountable for the work they do. As communities are made up of diverse groups with different interests and priorities, notably with regard to security, it is critical that wardens do not become too closely associated with particular sections within a community.

Activities in residential areas

Respondents in Halton Moor were asked a series of questions about how successful they judged neighbourhood wardens to be in undertaking a number of tasks. Just over half felt unable to make such a judgement due to their lack of knowledge about neighbourhood wardens and their work. Figure 15 presents the finding of those who proffered a judgement.

Figure 15: Success of neighbourhood wardens at certain activities (%)

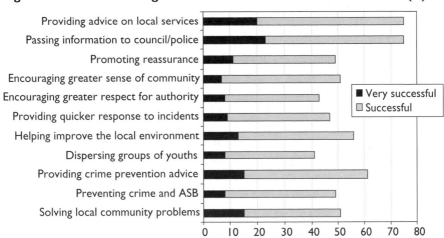

In descending order, the activities that residents felt wardens were the most successful at were passing on information about crime and anti-social behaviour to the police and council (75%); providing advice on local services and facilities (75%); providing crime prevention advice (61%); and helping improve the quality of the local environment (56%).

Respondents felt that the 'community rangers' (private security officers patrolling Foxwood) were most successful at passing information to the council and police (68%), followed by dispersing groups of local youths (49%), promoting reassurance (47%), providing a quicker response to incidents (46%) and improving the local environment (46%) (Figure 16). Respondents thought that the patrols were least successful at encouraging greater respect for authority (22%), followed by providing crime prevention advice (30%), providing advice on local services (31%), solving local community problems (32.5%) and encouraging a greater sense of community (34%).

Figure 16: Success of community rangers at certain activities (%)

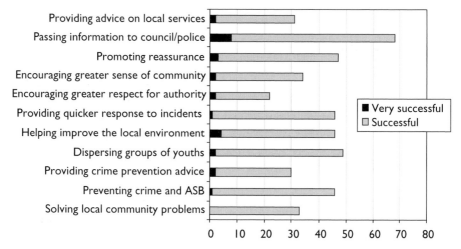

Improving communication with the public

Dedicated patrol officers who remain in post for a sufficient duration to become familiar to the local community and develop a sophisticated understanding of the areas in which they work can build up trust with local residents, businesses and visitors and local knowledge of the problems and resources within given localities. Ensuring continuity means not moving patrol officers from one location to the next or abstracting them to other duties, which will have an adverse impact on sustaining relations within the community. Dedicated patrol personnel can also provide good communication between the police and the policed.

Communication can be facilitated by:

- Enhanced accessibility through a local office from which patrol officers work, based in or close to frequented places or amenities – shopping, leisure, educational, health, business, etc – with convenient opening times. Such an operational base could be conjoined with other local (community safety) service providers under the same roof in a 'one-stop shop' (such as in Halton Moor). Where this is not possible, a drop-in base may prove an alternative option.
- Good quality public relations, publicising the names and contact details of individual officers (with photographs) in public places and local media outlets. Informing residents and businesses about the local partnership initiatives, their realistic aims and limitations, for example through meetings, newsletters and leaflets.

External and internal communications and marketing strategies are important in promoting public and professional understandings of plural policing strategies and in responding to particular media reports and incidents.

Community engagement

The research sites and initiatives studied all highlighted the importance of engaging with local residents and businesses, exploiting their knowledge about local crime and disorder problems and providing them with a stake in their own community policing efforts. Good community consultation at both strategic and operational levels was identified as important in establishing and maintaining community engagement, for example:

- Providing local people and businesses with accurate information on local crime and patrol activities, to allow local citizens knowledge of crime patterns in an understandable form and help build a constructive and informed relationship.
- Engaging with established business and community groups and facilitating dialogue with hard-to-reach and vulnerable groups, including asylum seekers, homeless persons, drug users and older and young people, as well as members of Black and minority ethnic communities.
- Involving personnel in key activities with vulnerable groups such as refugee and asylum support services, victim support and witness assistance programmes.
- Organising activities that seek to involve the community alongside policing personnel, such as 'community clear-up' days and other events with young people.

Dedicated patrol personnel can engage with different community groups and police audiences in ways that police officers find difficult given the variety of pressures on them. Moreover, wardens and private security officers often reflect better the diversity of communities they serve than police officers, particularly with regard to Black and minority ethnic representation. In this regard, CSOs afford a way of recruiting into the police significant numbers of traditionally under-represented groups, notably women and people from Black or minority ethnic communities. However, there is also a danger of creating a bifurcated body of policing personnel, with predominantly white police constables supported by a body of largely female and Black or minority ethnic colleagues in less well-paid civilian roles both within and outside the police organisation.

Responsiveness to local needs

Responsiveness to local needs and individual incidents or calls for assistance provides a form of direct accountability to local citizens. However, policing inevitably entails mediating between the potentially conflicting interests and demands of different sections of the population within a given locality.

- Local service-level agreements can provide a useful framework in which to manage local expectations and respond to local needs. It is important, however, that such local service-level agreements are genuinely tailored to the requirements of the local community rather than central organisational demands or government targets that may poorly reflect locally expressed needs.
- Providing monthly activity reports to local communities, business and beneficiaries on incidents and actions taken can provide useful feedback, foster community engagement and invest people with a sense of ownership.
- Structured community feedback – such as focus group interviews and surveys – can help to avoid problems escalating. Non-traditional methods of consultation may help elicit feedback from otherwise hard-to-reach groups within communities, such as young and older people.
- Enabling residents to provide confidential information to patrol personnel on problems, hot spots and potential solutions – such as a well-publicised dedicated telephone number or 'tasking box' – can encourage local participation and give people an investment and stake in their own policing activities.

Developing community cohesion

Wardens are well-placed to make quick impacts on improvements to the physical environment, which can produce instant benefits for local reassurance. Such endeavours can sit alongside longer-term community regeneration initiatives. Where community development is a priority, wardens are able to work with local young people in a diversionary capacity.

Visible figures of authority may act as intermediate institutions between the formal structures of police and local authorities on the one hand, and the informal institutions of civil society, such as families, schools, peer groups, businesses and community associations, on the other hand. As such, they may constitute the glue that binds people together and promotes social capital.

> Whereas physical capital refers to physical objects and human capital refers to the properties of individuals, social capital refers to connections among individuals – social networks and the norms of reciprocity and trustworthiness that arise from them. In that sense, social capital is closely related to what some have called 'civic virtue'. The difference is that 'social capital' calls attention to the fact that civic virtue is most powerful when embedded in a dense network of reciprocal social relations. A society of many virtuous but isolated individuals is not necessarily rich in social capital. (Putnam, 2000, p 19)

Wardens and other patrol personnel can assist in building social capital through networks and trust that facilitate coordination and cooperation for mutual benefit. Unlike other patrol personnel, wardens tend to be dedicated to fixed boundaries, allowing them to build significant relationships with the communities they serve. To a degree, this is also true of CSOs, but they tend to be deployed across wider areas, and move more frequently in line with wider policing priorities. However, as our Halton Moor site illustrated, wardens can also be moved around in line with wider council-determined priorities.

Neighbourhood wardens work particularly well in communities in which there are high rates of crime and ASB, high levels of distrust between residents and the police or a lack of collective efficacy, defined as "the linkage of mutual trust and the willingness to intervene for the common good" (Sampson et al, 1997, p 919). By contrast, neighbourhood wardens work less well in areas without a substantial residential population or where there are few visitors using public spaces (such as with the work of street wardens in city centres). This was certainly the experience with the ill-fated introduction of neighbourhood wardens into the Trafford Park Industrial Estate.

Patrol personnel can contribute to community cohesion in a number of ways (ODPM, 2004, p 80), through:

- bonding social capital: encouraging strong ties among groups of people that share similar values, interests and backgrounds;
- bridging social capital: facilitating strong bonds between different social groups within a community – between generations and cultural, ethnic and religious groups – and across communities;
- linking social capital: enhancing ties that connect people to local service providers, resources and formal organisations.

Wardens are particularly good at encouraging bonding and linking social capital, notably where communities are reasonably cohesive and have developed informal networks. Wardens in Halton Moor helped generate new resources for the area and linked residents into appropriate local services. Enhancing bridging social capital constitutes a particularly challenging aspect of wardens' work and one that should be further developed.

These different forms of social capital can work in mutually reinforcing, but also in competing, ways (see Figure 17). For example, linking social capital can foster intra-group bonding and inter-group bridging. However, bonding capital, by creating strong in-group loyalty and affective relations, may also create strong out-group antagonism within and between local communities, particularly given the fears and anxieties that security, crime and policing excite.

Wardens afford the capacity to foster approaches to local problems of order that exist beyond policing and security solutions alone, and afford the opportunity to tackle more fundamental social issues that often lie behind and inform these problems. They can help foster open, tolerant and inclusive communities by addressing inter-generational or ethnic conflict, whereas seeking solutions to problems of local order through a policing lens alone may serve to exacerbate residents' fears and solidify lines of difference within and between local communities.

Figure 17: Forms of social capital

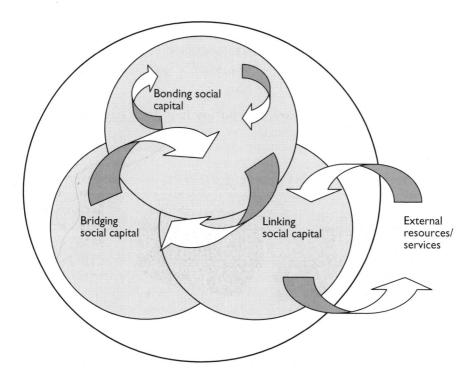

While other patrol personnel – private security and police – are able to contribute to community cohesion, this aspect of their work tends to be subsumed within a reassurance and patrol function. Simply responding to public demands for greater security through the provision of more security hardware and policing may fail to engage with, and negotiate the nature of, public demands and, in so doing, miss the opportunity to subject them to rational debate and local dialogue.

Community intelligence

A potential by-product of community engagement may be a greater willingness on the part of local communities to pass relevant information to the police via patrol personnel. Greater accessibility of CSOs, wardens and private security is likely to encourage an increased flow of useful information to the police from the public. In addition, the very presence of patrol personnel in public places them in a good position to observe and record incidents. It also enables them to monitor the 'traces' of crime and disorder on the local environment, namely physical indicators of some form of ASB, graffiti, broken glass, needles, litter, etc. As such, patrol personnel can act as additional 'eyes and ears' on the streets, collecting important community-level information and intelligence.

As intermediaries not directly associated with the police, neighbourhood wardens (and to a degree private security) are able to develop community-based relations that police officers would be unable to achieve. They can be seen as more approachable. Of those Halton Moor residents who expressed a view, 62% said that they would be likely to pass on information about local crime and ASB activities to the neighbourhood wardens (Figure 18).

Figure 18: Likelihood of passing on information to a neighbourhood warden in Halton Moor

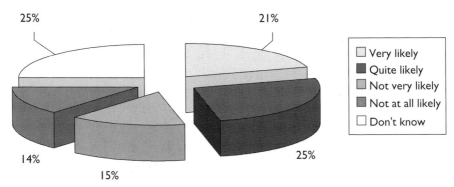

25%   21%

14%   25%

15%

Very likely
Quite likely
Not very likely
Not at all likely
Don't know

Moreover, 15% of those who offered an opinion said that they would be willing to pass on information to a neighbourhood warden that they would otherwise not tell the police. Interestingly, those who said they might do so spanned different age groups. This suggests that, for some, neighbourhood wardens can act as useful intermediaries in the collection of community intelligence about crime and disorder. Residents also felt that neighbourhood wardens can be more community-focused and build trust with residents:

> [Neighbourhood wardens] are more approachable than police. Wardens need to have more local knowledge than a PC. [The main benefit of wardens] is having more time to communicate with residents. (Halton Moor resident)

The arm's-length relationship between neighbourhood wardens and police can be simultaneously a benefit and a burden. For three quarters of residents surveyed on the Halton Moor estate, passing on information to the police or council was what they thought neighbourhood wardens were the most successful at. Yet, too close an association with the police can be problematic. Wardens need to balance their policing functions with their wider environmental and community engagement roles, such that the former does not undermine the latter.

Ambiguities surrounding the precise nature of this balance are reflected as much in central government thinking as in local practice:

> There's this sort of tension between how the Home Office see wardens and how the Office of the Deputy Prime Minister see them, where it sees the community safety role as just a little sub-set of the whole range of roles that wardens do. (Neighbourhood Wardens Team Manager)

Given the importance of personal relations that wardens are able to foster in communities:

- *Personalities matter:* Wardens bring personal experiences, skills and qualities to their work. As such, different wardens approach their work with differing styles. One consequence of this variation is that warden schemes differ considerably depending on the people working for them, leading to the experience that 'no two schemes are the same'.
- *Familiarity and detached neutrality are essential:* Wardens need to negotiate between championing community interests and an impartial mediator role that stands above the interests of groups within given communities. There is an ambiguity in that the more attached to or embedded within a community wardens are, the less likely they are to hold the required impartiality or 'detached stance' that constitutes a central value in establishing neutrality, as well as perceptions of fairness and legitimacy. There are dangers that wardens can become too familiar and closely associated with certain groups or interests.
- *Staff turnover can disrupt important social relations:* Where staff are moved or leave post this can adversely impact on relations within and between community members.

Private security officers on patrol in residential areas can also be the source of useful community intelligence. Figure 19 shows how likely respondents said they would be to give information about local crime or ASB activities to the private security community rangers in Foxwood. Of those who expressed a view, 73% said that they would be likely to pass on such information.

Figure 19: Likelihood of passing on information to community rangers in Foxwood

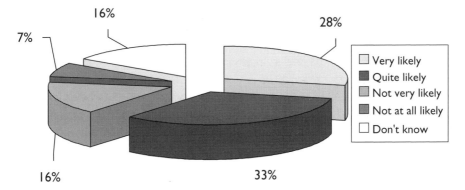

Moreover, 29% of those who offered an opinion said that they would be willing to pass on information to a community ranger that they would otherwise not tell the police. This suggests that, for some, community rangers can also act as intermediaries in the collection of community intelligence about crime and disorder.

Local knowledge and capacity

Local knowledge entails getting to know local businesses and residents, the relations between them, their capacity to support security endeavours and the diverse needs and policing challenges of the locality. Developing informed local knowledge takes time on the part of policing personnel and organisations, requiring them to build and sustain relations with businesses and residents. Inevitably, this is enhanced where individual staff are dedicated to specific areas and there is limited staff turnover.

In Halton Moor, of those residents who expressed a view in survey, 57% said that the local police and 56% said that neighbourhood wardens had a good understanding of the area. In Foxwood, of those who expressed a view, some 60% said that the local police and 52% said that community rangers had a good understanding of the area.

Where local patrols are not undermined by a rapid turnover of staff, policing personnel can potentially reconnect communities with local policing efforts and, as such, tap into and exploit local knowledge and capacity. Historically, the problem for private security providers has been the rapid turnover of staff, often fuelled by poor pay and conditions within the industry.

The research shows that in problem-solving endeavours, it is important that policing personnel engage and consult with local residents and businesses. Drawing on people's local resources and knowledge can significantly assist in community safety. Local people's own informal policing and security efforts can be nurtured and stimulated by plural policing personnel.

In seeking to access local knowledge policing agencies sometimes recruit personnel from within local communities. However, significant tensions overshadow the notion that policing personnel should live locally. As well as disrupting the extent to which policing is seen as impartial, it may deter policing actors from confronting conflictual situations. In York, a private security guard patrolling the Foxwood area was transferred to patrol another area of the city precisely because he lived locally. This was felt both to place him at risk of intimidation and raise potential conflicts of interest.

To encourage CSOs in Bradford to engage with and get to know their locality, police managers tasked them to visit local shops, businesses and offices within their beat areas, and to record each occasion they did so as part of their daily activities record. In the four months up to the end March 2004, CSOs in Bradford averaged more than 2,500 such visits per month (Figure 20). Of those CSOs surveyed, over three quarters (81%) said that they knew members of the public well, with whom they came into contact. However, less than half (46%) said that they approached members of the public very often.

Figure 20: Visits recorded by CSOs in Bradford (April 2003-January 2004)

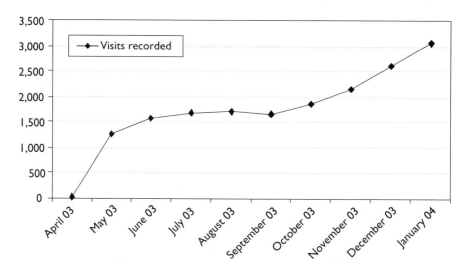

Despite problems of measurement, according to CSOs, this performance recording encouraged them actively to engage with local businesses, familiarise themselves with the area and collect community intelligence in the process. Related to this, CSOs have also worked actively with local shops to prevent them selling alcohol to underage drinkers and intoxicated people. This problem-solving approach may be responsible for the reduction in the number of alcohol-related incidents recorded in the city centre.

Legal powers

West Yorkshire Police was identified as one of the six initial forces piloting CSOs' powers of detention; a conditional power to be exercised if a person refuses to supply their name and address or those details provided are believed false. The power of detention lasts for a period of 30 minutes pending the arrival of a police constable (or the detained person being escorted to a police station)[3]. The research suggests that, in the initial stages of deployment, recruits were unfamiliar with the appropriate use of discretion and were likely to have too hasty a recourse to formal detention powers where other courses of action might have been more suitable. As a consequence, in the first four months of deployment, CSOs in Bradford exercised formal detention powers on average approximately 17 times per month (in total). Police managers were concerned about the high level of recourse to detention powers and arranged a collective meeting with CSOs to discuss the matter. Consequently, the use of detention powers declined significantly, to an average of just over five times per month over the subsequent eight months.

In 83% of cases, the detainee was subsequently arrested by a police officer, suggesting the appropriate use of detention powers by CSOs in that the incident was deemed serious enough to warrant arrest. The detainee was released after the arrival of a police officer in 9% of incidents and after arrival at a police station in a further 5%. Only in one incident was the detainee released because the time limit had been exceeded and in another incident the detainee absconded. According to the assessment of the detaining CSOs, most felt that, in the majority of incidents (63%), the use of the power made the intervention easier to deal with and a quarter said that it made no difference. However, only a minority (12%) said that they would not have dealt with the incident without the detention power. These findings are broadly in line with the national evaluation conducted by the Home Office (Singer, 2004).

The government's drive to enable patrol personnel, beyond sworn constables, to exercise certain limited legal powers with regard to disorder and ASB marks a significant development in seeking to harness the capacity of plural policing. Through community safety accreditation schemes, wardens and private security

---

[3] Should a constable not arrive within this period, the detainee must be released.

personnel can be given limited legal powers, and the government is currently proposing to expand the range of powers available to CSOs as set out in *Policing: Modernising police powers to meet community needs* (Home Office, 2004c) and incorporated in the current Serious Organised Crime and Police Bill. Extending legal powers to plural policing personnel, however, does have significant drawbacks and challenges:

- It may undermine the nature of their role, fostering a 'mission creep' away from reassurance patrol towards law enforcement.
- It may transform the nature of relations between patrol personnel and the public by drawing them into more adversarial relations.
- By raising the threshold of confrontation and conflict, it may place patrol personnel in more dangerous environments and risky situations.
- Interrelatedly, it may encourage a 'powers creep', whereby patrol personnel necessitate more powers as they are drawn into shifting roles, relations with the public and different situations.
- The use of legal powers raises questions concerning individual human rights, and requires robust procedures for ensuring that powers are appropriately used.
- By necessity, the provision of additional powers also demands considerably more training to ensure the appropriate use of those powers. This, of itself, may not be problematic but may question why the powers are not being exercised by sworn police officers.

Ultimately, the allocation of increased powers to certain patrol personnel can further blur the distinction between types of patrol officer and can add to public uncertainties and confusion.

The research highlights concerns that giving patrol personnel legal powers (or in the case of CSOs more legal powers), particularly to issue fixed penalty notices, may undermine their wider tasks, notably engaging with the local community and participating in problem-solving endeavours. The availability of formal and coercive legal powers may reduce their application of powers of persuasion and negotiation, which ultimately are the patrol officer's most potent means of inducing compliance.

Additional powers for CSOs

While policing is ultimately bound up with recourse to formal coercive power – the policing of, and decisions over, people – policing personnel rely on a certain degree of 'quasi-voluntary compliance' or 'consent' on the part of citizens. Such consensual or compliance policing is not purely self-interested or instrumental but also has a normative base, strongly linked to perceptions of legitimacy. This is important because the coercive powers of police are themselves limited and only used as an option of last resort. It is only if compliance breaks down that recourse to coercive legal powers is required.

Effective CSOs, like police officers more generally, draw on the authority of their office and their personal and craft skills in handling people rather than coercive powers. Given the limits of coercive power, policing personnel must depend on 'consensual' deference to their decisions by most of the people with whom they most regularly interact. Granting CSOs more coercive powers may encourage them to rely less on the construction of consent, instead preferring to resort to the apparently easier reliance on coercion or enforcement. Moreover, recourse to legal powers may undermine the legitimacy of officers' authority in the eyes of the public. It may produce a more antagonistic relationship between the officers and the local people policed. As policing researchers have long noted, the preservation of good order may often require the non-enforcement of laws and the exercise of discretion in recourse to legal powers (Bittner, 1967).

One comparison frequently drawn in our West Yorkshire focus group interviews was with the very different role of traffic wardens, whose essential task is largely an enforcement one through issuing fixed penalty notices. This affects both the relationship between public and traffic wardens and the respect with which traffic wardens are held by the public. A West Yorkshire Police sergeant made this point explicitly:

> If you give [CSOs] the powers to give out tickets all the time, they will create a negative image with the public. The public doesn't like traffic wardens and CSOs will find themselves in a catch-22 situation.

Additional powers for wardens

Calls for patrol personnel to be given additional powers have become a key element of government policy, as foreshadowed by the proposed Clean Neighbourhoods and Environment Bill. According to our research, similar but ambiguous calls are also reflected among members of the public. This has particularly been the case with regard to neighbourhood wardens. Our research found that many residents appeared inconsistent in their views about wardens, on the one hand appreciating the community-based nature of their role and, on the other hand, wanting them to be given more powers and to work later in the evenings and at weekends, because these were the times at which the greatest perceived threats to security occurred. A significant majority (82%) of Halton Moor survey respondents agreed that wardens should be given more powers to deal with anti-social behaviour. Yet, the following resident, among others, noted:

> Too many powers given to the wardens may cause people to avoid approaching or discussing problems with the wardens if they are seen to be too closely linked with the police. (Halton Moor resident)

Hence, there are dangers in constructing the warden's role primarily in policing or security terms. To do so is likely to see wardens increasingly drawn into law enforcement activities that place them in situations of conflict, possibly undermining their capacity to perform other non-policing functions. The more that a community's problems are seen through a security lens, the more that policing, exclusion and law and order solutions are likely to be prioritised.

This tension between a policing model of wardens with extra powers and a more community-focused role in which wardens have no extra powers was highlighted by the warden on the Halton Moor estate, as was the uncertainty over which model is most appropriate:

> The first model of a warden would be to have no powers of intervention, no powers of arrest, have a visible uniform that is different from the police and security. So one wouldn't have a role where they'd be directly intervening in the community to address crime and the reduction of crime in that sense. How they would be effective would be by sharing information in partnership with other agencies.... The other role is a community support officer role, which does have powers of intervention to a limited degree, does have powers of arrest to a limited degree, does have a uniform that is visibly recognisable as part of the police. So, I think that the argument we have as wardens is with our senior management as well as other people in the community, ie, politicians and such like. What do you want us to do, which role do you want us to fulfil? Either it'll be one or the other. We can't be both. Now with the formation of community support officers, we feel that it should swing totally away from that model. It should be divided and the community should be given information to recognise what our role is and what the community support officer role is.' (Halton Moor warden)

This warden echoes wider concerns over the blurring of roles and the need for a clearer division of labour so as to address public confusion.

The danger is the more that wardens are drawn towards a policing focus, the more they may be perceived as less capable 'quasi'-police officers, given their lack of additional powers, the fact that they work during the day and their limited institutional support. It is not surprising therefore, in areas where neighbourhood wardens are being pulled (by resident demands and political pressure) into more security-focused roles, that their raison d'être may be weakened. Hence, when asked, half of the Halton Moor respondents to the survey agreed that they would prefer a CSO rather than a neighbourhood warden patrolling the estate, whereas just over a quarter (26%) disagreed. In some senses, this could be read as a considerable vote of confidence for the wardens' role, as elsewhere in Leeds local councillors under perceived pressure from electors voted to transfer local authority devolved funding from wardens to CSOs.

Additional powers for private security personnel

Given the embryonic stage of development of the private security regulatory regime, the principal concern with additional powers for security personnel relates to potential misuse and infringements of individual rights. While the Independent Police Complaints Commission oversees the conduct of police employees, there are different arrangements of varying degrees of efficacy in place with regard to wardens and private security personnel. The legislation requires that employers of accredited persons make suitable arrangements to supervise the use of their conferred powers when carrying out community safety functions, including satisfactory arrangements for handling complaints. However, the adequacy of these arrangements is likely to be considerably uneven. The legislation specifically seeks to remove liability from the police for any unlawful conduct that may take place in the performance of policing work by accredited officers. Rather, this should fall on their employers.

Equipment

To a certain extent, similar concerns to those raised above with regard to increased legal powers can arise with regard to providing patrol personnel with greater personal equipment and resort to technology. While the case for patrol personnel to be well protected in terms of their own personal safety is crucial, nevertheless, supplying them with some equipment – such as batons, CS gas spray or handcuffs in the case of CSOs – may alter the way in which they interact with the public. They may come to rely on such equipment in ways that can affect public perception of them and may lead them into more dangerous situations.

Impact of public–private partnerships on private security

Our research highlights significant evidence of a 'cross-fertilisation' effect where plural policing bodies work in close partnerships, especially where this occurs at an operational level. Close cooperation encourages and facilitates a merging (and borrowing) of public and private styles of policing, as well as different cultural sensibilities to the delivery of policing and order maintenance. This 'cross-fertilisation' effect works both on the police and private security.

Traditionally, commercial security has tended to prioritise strategies that are primarily instrumental in their focus on loss prevention and risk reduction, while the public police have been noted for their emphasis on moral concerns with law enforcement or the detection, prosecution and conviction of criminals (Shearing and Stenning, 1981). This is because private security firms have commercial interests to attend to and protect that diverge significantly from those of public prosecution.

Furthermore, private security has been distinguished by a proactive rather than reactive approach to problem solving that has marked public policing. Yet, our research suggests that this rather stark contrast, while reflecting important enduring elements in different styles of policing, oversimplifies the nature of plural policing where cooperation and partnership working are evident. The research highlights a number of impacts of close partnership arrangements on private security.

Encourages greater awareness and responsibility on the part of businesses, groups and individuals for managing crime: Partnerships can foster greater awareness on the part of businesses and citizens of their responsibilities for their own crime prevention and safety. This is particularly true for many bigger businesses and retail outlets, for which stock loss is not seen as a major issue, but merely a hazard of business enterprise. Public–private partnerships can encourage businesses to examine the criminal opportunities that their operations provide or facilitate and reduce the opportunities for crime.

Inherent within the MetroCentre initiative was a desire to encourage stores to adopt greater responsibility with regard to their own crime prevention, not only in so far as it impacted on their own stock and profit margins, but also with regard to wider implications (that is, for neighbouring businesses). One strategy used to encourage this responsibility involved contracted police officers proactively engaging with stores and their personnel. Officers were given the task of recruiting stores to the partnership initiative. As a lever, police began to inform stores and outlets that higher priority status would be accorded to those that actively sought to reduce crime opportunities and participated in crime prevention initiatives.

The findings of our survey of retailers in the MetroCentre show that a significant number of retailers said their awareness of security within the confines of their own unit/store had increased as a consequence of the initiative (41%). Moreover, a quarter of retailers said that they had increased the nature of in-house security measures. Retailers also acknowledged a greater awareness of security issues within the wider MetroCentre as a result of the policing initiative (54%).

Encourages private security to manage incidents themselves or intervene before requiring police intervention: One of the explicit aims of some partnerships is to reduce the involvement of the police and public prosecution by forms of early intervention. For example, the MetroCentre initiative sought to encourage decisions not to arrest. Early on, a protocol was drawn up by Northumbria Police solicitors stating that this objective was to ensure that resources were directed more to prevention of crime than crime detection. St James' Security (the private security provider contracted to patrol the common areas in the MetroCentre) was encouraged not to involve the police or call for police assistance in relation to minor incidents (small, low-value thefts). Instead, security staff were encouraged to contact the CCTV control room in the Management Centre and for an image of the 'offender' to be saved for inclusion on an 'offenders' database. If the same person is caught reoffending or causing trouble, the police will be called to intervene. This gives the offender 'one chance' and does not result in a recorded crime incident.

Police tend to regard security staff in terms of their capacity to deter crime before it happens (thus negating the need for police involvement) rather than involve the police in arrests. In this sense, the police view uniformed in-store guards more favourably than covert in-store detectives. This is also true of the MetroCentre 'X-ray team' (a covert private, in-house security team). To encourage 'deterrence' rather than apprehension, the police arranged for letters of commendation for security staff who successfully deterred offenders (rather than call police assistance). The police sergeant differentiated between 'good' and 'bad' in-house security, dependent on how much work they created for the police; the less work the better.

The fact that the MetroCentre retailers are paying for police officers means that they have a direct incentive not to tie up those police officers in time-consuming arrests, as they then have less time to provide visible reassurance. As such, there is a consensus among police, security and MetroCentre management that the police should not arrest people for all crimes – notably where they are of a trivial nature – as this is viewed as a waste of police resources in processing such cases. Nevertheless, some of the larger stores viewed 'success' within a framework of arrests. Where stores had a policy always to call for police assistance, the partnership sought to challenge and change this approach. Nevertheless, some security staff (in-store and St James' staff) did not necessarily share the view that the police should only be used selectively.

Encourages private security to adopt wider 'quasi-public' functions: As well as policing in public and 'quasi-public' spaces (private property to which the public has liberal access), private security is increasingly taking on wider, quasi-public functions, particularly where they are drawn into partnerships with public organisations. This includes:

- Passing on information, incident reports, CCTV footage to the police and other public authorities. As well as working with the police to prosecute crime and solve local crime-related problems that extend beyond narrow private interests, a surveillance or 'eyes and ears' function of private security was to be found to a lesser or greater degree in all the research sites.
- Disseminating information from public authorities to relevant private organisations and businesses for crime prevention and detection purposes. In most of the sites the police provided private security with local intelligence on known and suspected offenders. For example, in the Liverpool Gold Zones, private security staff were provided with information and photographs of individuals wanted on warrant or who were the subject of court orders. Business

Crime Direct (BCD) [4] also developed close links with the newly formed Truancy Team, which informs them about and involves them in truancy sweeps of the city centre.

- Responding to incidents as directed by the public police. For example, in York the private security patrols are regularly directed by police control room staff to attend low-level incidents, notably relating to groups of youths gathering in public places. This use of private security staff tended to be more pronounced where police resources are acutely stretched, but was largely ad hoc and operated without any formal protocols.

- Working in public places beyond the immediate geographic boundaries of the 'private' contracted area. For example, the private security company operating community ranger patrols in Foxwood responded to calls for assistance on their Freephone number, even where these related to incidents outside their designated areas. While this activity may be stimulated more by public relations benefits, nevertheless, it draws private patrols into wider security concerns. However, as the following private security manager notes, this public spiritedness has its limits:

> What we don't want is, if somebody from Micklegate rings up with a problem, we don't want to say to them 'sorry but you're two streets off the coverage', and we don't say that to them to be honest, we do respond. But we don't then want everybody in Micklegate to start ringing through to our 0800 number and start taking the services off Foxwood. So we don't want to be restricted in areas in terms of well, I'm sorry, we can't go into your area because you don't participate in the scheme. (Private security manager)

In addition, the MetroCentre security staff worked with Northumbria Police to help set up partnerships with retail crime prevention organisations in Newcastle, Gateshead, Durham and Cleveland. MetroCentre security has also participated in schemes to encourage 'pro-social' behaviour among young people through incentive schemes, such as the SMART card initiative to promote 'good citizenship'. This is a good example of the elision between public values and private concerns, as the MetroCentre is clearly keen to welcome 'good consumers' while preventing security risks.

- Encouraging businesses to share information on crime, individuals who present risks and exclusions. In the Liverpool Gold Zones, the government-funded BCD encouraged in-house, retail private security to deal with shop thieves in a more organised manner in which information is shared. BCD reported that in many instances of theft, security personnel were dealing in isolation with offenders by simply excluding them from their own premises. BCD encouraged sharing

---

[4] BCD is a government backed initiative, attached to Liverpool Chamber of Commerce, with the aim of reducing crime against businesses. See www.businesscrimedirect.org.uk

information on exclusions, so that individuals excluded from one business could also be excluded from all cooperating stores. Similarly, the MetroCentre partnership worked hard to develop shared policies of exclusions within the centre. Notably, MetroLand (a leisure theme park in the MetroCentre), with its own security, had traditionally been reluctant to allow MetroCentre security to enter MetroLand premises and would eject undesirable people from MetroLand, displacing troublemakers into the rest of the centre. MetroCentre management developed a policy with the police whereby MetroLand security inform St James staff before they eject people so that St James' officers can 'meet them' and escort the individuals from the centre. MetroLand has its own policy on exclusions but now there is coordination. Individuals banned from MetroLand are also banned from the MetroCentre and vice versa.

Impact of public–private partnerships on the police

In addition, the research identified a number of impacts of close partnership working on the police.

A greater emphasis on proactive crime prevention, risk and loss minimisation: Contracted police officers within the MetroCentre have worked with the centre and local schools to provide a discount card scheme for well-behaved pupils. They have also liaised with the local Youth Offending Team to undertake supervised community service around the site. The SMART card initiative, aimed at seven- to 17-year-old youths, was designed to reward good behaviour with points that could be used in shops in the MetroCentre. Points could also be removed for bad behaviour. Outlets able to award and remove points were the MetroCentre, police and local participating schools.

A more significant role for the police as repositories of crime-related information: A central element of plural policing interactions revolves around information exchange. In this, the public police play a pivotal role as 'information brokers', both as the recipients and providers of crime-related information. Their function constitutes collating, analysing and disseminating information in liaison with other policing bodies. The role of Merseyside Police in seconding an officer to BCD to process and manage a database of offenders on behalf of its members is evidence of this development. As a result, the police role facilitated private security personnel to manage offenders by excluding them from their stores. Similarly, on Trafford Park the police undertook a key role in disseminating crime intelligence to wardens and private security.

As Ericson and Haggerty (1997) have noted, policing is increasingly information-driven and relations between plural policing bodies are often concerned with negotiating information exchange. 'Communications policing' lies at the heart of many partnership arrangements and the police have increasingly taken on an 'information-brokering' role: collating, analysing and disseminating information in liaison with other policing bodies. However, the nature and extent of information exchange has tended to be overstated (both by academics and police managers) in relation to England and Wales.

Opportunities for the police to work creatively beyond the confines of normal policing where they are subcontracted to private interests: The contracted community beat managers (CBMs) in the MetroCentre were not merely tied to reactive duties. They were not 'slaves to the radio', as one CBM described it. As such, they were able to dedicate significant time to high-visibility reassurance patrols. Furthermore, CBMs were able to work beyond the confines of normal police constables. For example, they actively promoted the Crime and Disorder Watch scheme to retailers. There was a strong emphasis on building partnerships and working relationships with retailers. The CBMs were an important 'clubbing' resource, encouraging individual retailers to adopt a broader mentality and concern beyond the narrow instrumental confines of the security of their own private 'space'. They were able to encourage and create important social capital in the development of collective security. They did so by networking with retailers – in ways that St James' security was unable to do, in part, because the police were seen as 'honest brokers'. In addition, the police acted as collective information providers/analysts for the purpose of intelligence-led policing (targeting hot spots, suspects and known offenders – what one CBM described as 'predictive policing'). The MetroCentre and St James also contributed significantly to the information collection and databases within the centre.

The growing role of exclusion

Exclusion has increasingly become a dominant means of managing collective security problems in private, quasi-public and public places. Exclusion is one of the principal tools inherent in the ownership of private property (von Hirsch and Shearing, 2000; Wakefield, 2003). Recent case law suggests that in relation to the UK private property vests an almost unqualified common-law privilege to exclude or eject strangers, without the necessity for good reason or objective rational justification (*CIN Properties Ltd v Rawlins [1995] 2 EGLR 130* and *Appleby and Others v The United Kingdom, Application No 44306/98*). Consequently, security and police operating in shopping malls such as the MetroCentre in Gateshead deploy a variety of informal and formal modes of exclusion and expulsion. The most routine form of exclusion is ejection of perceived 'undesirables' from the premises on the basis of private property rights asserting a civil trespass order. Those who are 'not good for the image' of The Centre are 'asked to leave' as a type of pre-emptive exclusion of those who have no perceived commercial value or who are 'seen not to belong'. At a second tier, more formal 'exclusion notices' are sent by Centre management and categorised either for 'crime' or 'disorder' purposes. Records and images are kept and policed through the extensive CCTV system and the large number of security guards and contracted police officers operating throughout the shopping malls. Banning orders usually last for 12 months. If a person breaks an exclusion notice, they are warned that they are liable to be sued for trespass.

However, not all forms of exclusion were uniformly welcomed by private businesses. Some blanket exclusion strategies were seen as unhelpful by retailers. For example, in the MetroCentre, at one point the police imposed a curfew on unaccompanied youths under 18, half an hour after the stores had closed, but when some of the leisure outlets remained open. Certain businesses complained about the potential negative impact on their profits, emphasising that they want to exclude 'troublemakers', not potentially 'good consumers'.

In addition to these forms of 'private justice', shopping malls and city centre managers can and do resort to the courts and criminal justice agencies for exclusions, either in the form of an exclusion order, an ASBO, exclusions attached to bail conditions or exclusions as part of a youth offender contract or anti-social behaviour contract. Thus in Liverpool, BCD has forged close links with the local Anti-Social Behaviour Unit and was considering nominating certain persistent offenders for an ASBO. It also had very close links with the Youth Offending Service, which negotiates contracts with young offenders on a referral order. It encouraged the use of exclusion from certain stores in the city centre as an aspect of such contracts.

According to private security managers, given the considerable time and effort involved in formal exclusions through the courts, they often prefer the informality and discretion of their own exclusion notices. They tend only to rely on formal exclusion orders and ASBOs when informal means have been unsuccessful and/or an offence has been committed. Hence, recourse to the public courts is reserved for individuals who do not comply with 'private' methods of exclusion or where these have somehow failed. Importantly, in the MetroCentre, private security officers enforce informal exclusion notices rather than the contracted police. Otherwise this 'may damage the police image of impartiality', as one security manager noted.

Analogous modes of exclusion have also been introduced in recent years in relation to public places, the most notable being the ASBO, introduced by Section 1 of the 1998 Crime and Disorder Act. After a degree of reluctance on the part of local police and councils to use the new order, and on the back of chastisement from government, ASBOs have now become a significant and increasingly used tool in the policing of public spaces (Home Office, 2004a, p 50). Across England and Wales, more than 2,400 ASBOs have been issued since they were introduced in April 1999, with 1,323 taken out in the year to March 2004[5]. For local councils and

---

[5] Three of the cities in which our research sites have been located have figured prominently in the use of ASBOS: 422 issued in Greater Manchester since 1999, up 232% since 31 March 2003; 59 issued in Liverpool, up 139%; and 122 issued in Leeds, up 430%.

the police, sometimes in consultation with private authorities, ASBOs represent a novel way of managing low-level disorder and reasonably serious criminality. The lower evidentiary burdens that accompany a civil order supported by criminal sanctions (if breached) and the much broader range of restrictions that ASBOs afford in relation to behaviour, activities, places and people, make ASBOs attractive to public and private authorities as a means of governing conduct. In addition, the absence of press-reporting restrictions enables the use of local media to promote deterrence through the public shaming of individuals and as a means of encouraging ordinary citizens and businesses to police any exclusions and restrictions granted under an order. Local newspapers in the research sites assisted these endeavours by publishing names and photographs in prominent places.

Exclusions from certain public and private places are also being written into acceptable behaviour contracts and youth offender contracts. More recently, Part 4 of the 2003 Anti-Social Behaviour Act creates a power to disperse groups of two or more people (section 30). With local authority agreement, a senior police officer can designate an area where there is believed to be persistent anti-social behaviour and a problem with groups causing intimidation. Once a senior police officer and the local authority have agreed to designate an area, they must publish that fact in a local newspaper or through notices, and it can be designated for up to six months. In these areas, police and CSOs will have a power to disperse groups where their presence or behaviour has resulted, or is likely to result, in a member of the public being harassed, intimidated, alarmed or distressed. The individuals can then be excluded from a specified area for up to 24 hours.

This development formalises a policing strategy used, to varying degrees, by both private security and public police. Throughout the research, private security officers in York sought to disperse groups of youths whose presence in public spaces intimidated certain residents. Sometimes officers were summoned by residents. On other occasions, they were tasked via the police radio to attend locations where groups of youths were gathering. However, officers' attempts to disperse such groups were met with varied success.

Security dilemmas

There are ambiguities and tensions surrounding the public image of security, visible authority and policing. Security operates at the level of perceptions and hence processes of impression management are vital to presenting places as secure environments.

First, not all crime prevention initiatives are seen by all parties as inevitably desirable, particularly if they might involve adverse publicity. In the MetroCentre, the police wanted to issue a media release warning shoppers to watch out for bag snatches and purse thefts in the centre and also to erect a billboard warning of vehicle crime. Both these strategies were not seen as desirable and were blocked by the centre management as it was thought that they would give the impression that the centre is targeted by criminals and that shoppers might be particularly vulnerable, and that such strategies were not conducive to encouraging 'safe shopping'.

To a considerable degree, the effectiveness of policing and security is less important than their role in the production of organised legitimate symbols of 'orderly environments'. However, security and policing present something of a dichotomy: they can both reassure and excite anxieties. Focus group interviews regarding the work of CSOs in Bradford highlighted the ambiguous line that policing treads, in public perceptions, between reassurance and heightened anxieties. A number of respondents suggested that the sight of too many uniformed officers made them feel that there was something to be feared. This was particularly salient in the light of sensitivities over possible terrorist attacks. Symbols of security can remind us of our insecurities.

It is for this precise reason that some leisure outlets and retail units prefer not to associate themselves too closely with overt security, for fear that potential customers may be put off by the impression that this may give about a place being insecure, hence the need for security. For example, MetroLand does not have officially titled security officers. Rather, security is a latent function of all employees, albeit some more than others. In part, this is because MetroLand managers are wary of presenting an image of a place where security is necessary as it may make customers feel that the premises are unsafe:

> We don't have them in uniform, we don't have them in security uniforms. We have our own uniforms. And the reason for that is because we don't want a high presence of security. We don't want to look as if we need a high presence of security because that tends to make people think. There's two ways of looking at it. You either feel very secure or you think there's a problem and that's why you've got extra security. (MetroLand manager)

Visible security measures may fly in the face of commercial imperatives, as noted by a police crime reduction officer working on the Trafford Park Industrial Estate:

> From our perspective, we may say there is a need for this company to put this type of fence around their property in order to prevent their property being broken into. The problem is that the company may be very conscious of its public image. They may be conscious that putting a 2.3-metre palisade fence round their site may actually create an image which is negative to some potential clients and customers and that we should look for possibly softer alternatives.

Where the police have worked in partnership with businesses, they have been forced to acknowledge the importance of public image and work with commercial sensitivities concerning perceptions of security, as the following police officer at the MetroCentre appreciated:

> It's important we recognise that the MetroCentre have a much greater concern for their image, for the power of PR, and advertising, than perhaps we're used to dealing with. They want to avoid bad PR at all costs. I think in the past there have been difficulties ... where we wanted to put up notice boards saying 'look after your valuables, watch where you park in the MetroCentre', and that sort of activity just seems absolutely impossible because you can imagine the negative impact they would see that having.

Security, therefore, is double-edged; it operates at both levels of perception and reality. As an intangible, selling security presents challenges:

> Two big problems you have when delivering manned security services are: first, the better you are at it, the less there appears to be a need for it; and the second thing is that it has to be possible, the more you put in security measures, the more restricting it becomes to other people. So it's getting the balance – security must be understood and appreciated, unpredictable but reliable. (Senior security industry representative)

4

Public reassurance

Providing reassurance

Perceptions of safety are seen as crucial in attracting people and businesses to different locations, be they shopping centres, residential areas or industrial parks. Visible patrol personnel have become a key element in presenting a place as a secure environment. They are tangible symbols of authority and control, helping to portray the image of a place as secure and safe. In all the sites in our research, security (notably in the form of patrol personnel) was intimately connected with strategies for urban regeneration and renaissance. One of the explicit motivating factors behind the Trafford Park security initiative was concern that businesses might relocate away from the park, in part due to security fears. Similarly, politicians and business people involved in the Gold Zones initiative in Liverpool were unambiguous about the need to reposition the city in an international economy as a safe and vibrant place to do business[1]. Consequently, city centre managers and urban developers seeking to lure visitors and capital increasingly look to security systems and visible guarding as 'magnets' for regeneration (Minton, 2002). Nevertheless, reassurance is a complex product of subjective perceptions as well as objective crime-related risks.

Community support officers and reassurance

Community support officers (CSOs) can make a tangible difference to public reassurance. In Bradford city centre, CSOs were able to dedicate more than four fifths of their time to being out of the police station on visible patrols. The average time spent by CSOs on patrol between 1 April 2003 and the end of February 2004 was 80% in Bradford (Figure 21). This has been crucial to their success. Importantly, the proportion of time spent on visible patrol did not decrease during this period, but rather increased slightly (to an average of 82% in the last six months). This reflects the manner in which West Yorkshire Police successfully ring-fenced CSOs to specific patrol duties, in dedicated places and at specified times. They resisted pressures to use CSOs as a generic resource to fill service gaps within the organisation, which might have drawn them away from visible patrols.

---

[1] Similar sentiments underpinned Liverpool's successful bid to become the European Capital of Culture for 2008.

Figure 21: Percentage of time on visible patrol (April 2003-February 2004)

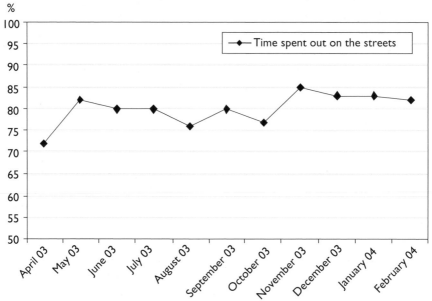

This 'visibility dividend' associated with CSOs contrasts starkly with the estimated 43% of a police constable's time spent on the streets (PA Consulting Group, 2001). Unlike CSOs, most of police officer time out of the station is spent dealing with incidents and making enquiries, while only 17% of police officer time is spent on reassurance patrols. Furthermore, police officer patrols are largely conducted from vehicles, in part because officers need to be able to respond rapidly to priority incidents.

As specialist patrol personnel with limited powers, CSOs are freed from most of the pressures that serve to abstract constables from dedicated local patrols. CSOs are not subject to the 'tyranny of the radio', as one interviewee described the reactive burdens on police constables. Instead, they are able to dedicate themselves to the policing of given localities in accordance with the community policing ideal that the British police have long sought but rarely realised.

The research highlights that patrol is not an end in itself, but rather a means to an end. It is not just the presence of uniformed patrol officers alone that influences public confidence and fosters reassurance, but also the manner with which they interact with the public. A central challenge, therefore, is to ensure that CSOs and other patrol personnel 'patrol with a purpose', supplementing visible presence with other activities including proactive crime prevention, intelligence gathering and community engagement.

We encountered concerns that CSOs were sometimes uncertain what to do beyond walking their beat as a kind of 'reassurance beacon' or 'mobile scarecrow', phrases used by CSOs themselves. Furthermore, patrolling in pairs can act as a barrier to community engagement[2]. Members of the public mentioned finding it off-putting to see CSOs apparently more concerned with their personal conversations (with their colleagues) than with engaging outwardly with their surroundings and interacting with the public. CSOs deep in conversation can inadvertently send out the message that 'we do not wish to be disturbed'.

In interview, some members of the public differentiated between the immediate reassurance value of patrol officers in uniform provided by their visible presence, and the capacity of patrol officers to deal with specific incidents, which was seen to have implications for their longer-term reassurance. One focus group interviewee elaborated:

> That for me is why this training issue of a fully qualified policeman really matters because if you say public reassurance you can also think long-term reassurance and that to me is where there's fully qualified policemen who work with people, who are much more senior, who've been around the block before, who know how to diffuse situations, not inflame them. My fear, I suppose, about an underqualified person, is that they can actually inflame a situation.

Most interviewees had not seen a patrol officer deal with a confrontational situation and were therefore uncertain as to how these might be handled. Where they had witnessed the successful negotiation of such situations, individuals said that they found this reassuring. As such, it is not just the presence of uniformed patrol officers that makes a difference, but also the way in which officers act and interact with members of the public that influences confidence and fosters reassurance. It was precisely this that led the following interviewee to suggest that private security guards might be more reassuring than CSOs:

> I feel more safe with a security guard in a shop because I've seen them do the job quite a lot and they always catch the person but none of these [CSOs], I've never actually seen them in a situation where they've caught anybody.

This reinforces previous research findings demonstrating that the way in which members of the public experience the regulatory activities of the police and other officials informs their perceptions of legitimacy and confidence in them (Tyler, 1998).

Focus groups with members of the public suggest that they invest a significant degree of both instrumental and symbolic authority in police personnel on the

---

[2] CSOs in Bradford often patrolled on their own, but paired up for evening and night-time duties.

basis of at least two commonly held beliefs. First, CSOs along with other police personnel are supported by, and linked into, a large, resourceful organisation that is able to respond rapidly and effectively to emergencies. Second, police personnel are assumed to conform to certain standards of professionalism – of skills and competencies – and of ethical conduct on the basis of selection, recruitment, training and supervision procedures.

In order to maintain public confidence, it is important that CSOs, in their public interactions, and the police organisation in its support of them, live up to these expectations. As CSOs increasingly become the public face of the police, it is imperative that they conform to the highest possible standards of ethical and professional policing in their public interactions, dispositions and attitudes. It is only under these conditions that CSOs will be able to deliver long-term public reassurance, beyond the immediacy of a visible officer in a uniform, and fulfil public expectations of them.

Analyses of maps deriving from surveys of public perceptions of fearful and safe places and recorded crime highlight the following (Crawford et al, 2004):

- Public perceptions of insecurity do not necessarily or neatly correspond with recorded crime risks. Recorded crime hot spots and public fear of crime hot spots are not always coterminous. Hence, public reassurance in part is concerned with subjective perceptions that connect with the symbolic and communicative functions of policing patrols and security.
- It is wrong to make assumptions about what matters to the different members of the public in the deployment of visible patrol officers. Changing public perceptions about order and safety is a qualitatively different task to crime fighting.
- Reassurance is not merely the product of dedicated police patrols but also connects with the work of other agencies and organisations as well as the presence or absence of other 'capable guardians', be they visible patrol personnel, non-security staff, residents or passers-by. The presence in city centres of large numbers of people, security guards and semi-official personnel may reduce the relative reassurance value of police patrols.

In the early stages of CSO deployment, their community engagement and problem-solving activities were less well developed. In part, this stemmed from the complex nature of the communities that comprise the city centre of Bradford. Nevertheless, over time, CSOs began to grapple with these challenges.

Where wardens are also working in a neighbourhood, CSOs can usefully link them into the police organisation, which for some wardens can otherwise seem very remote and inaccessible, as the warden on the Halton Moor estate noted:

> The police don't make an effort to contact the warden when they're on the warden's area. They don't automatically say, 'well I must contact the warden and find out what's going on'. It's generally we who have to try and find them. But if you've got community support officers on there, you've got a better link. Every day you can meet up and walk round the estate together and identify different issues and you'll know they're going to be there on a regular basis.

The future development of CSOs in part depends on an understanding of the intrinsic nature of the role. Crudely put, there are two essential models of the CSO function that implicitly or explicitly inform most assumptions:

The 'junior police officer' model: Here, CSOs are seen as a supplementary resource to be used by the police organisation to release police officers from time-consuming, minor and less serious tasks. They allow police officers to concentrate their activities on high-volume and more serious crime and to respond to emergencies. This model may entail CSOs performing tasks from which police officers have generally withdrawn, such as patrol, but also other low-level duties, such as attending a range of minor criminal incidents, undertaking focused investigation/ interview, static guarding of buildings/crime scenes, traffic duties, the investigation of sudden deaths or victim contact work. As such, CSOs are seen as a flexible new response to the high level of demand that restricts the activities of contemporary police forces. This model reflects a more fluid division of labour between CSOs and police officers.

The 'dedicated patrol officer' model: Here, the CSO is seen as a new breed of officer dedicated to providing reassurance to the public through high-visibility patrol. To deliver reassurance, CSOs need to be deployed so that they are seen by the public to be accessible, knowledgeable and visible. For this model to be most effective, CSOs need to develop an understanding of, and familiarity with, the people, problems and places they patrol. To deliver this model, CSOs should not be drawn into tasks that detract from their high-visibility role or that make them less accessible to the public. As such, CSOs are a response to heightened public anxieties regarding crime, disorder and anti-social behaviour, demands for visible policing and public disquiet about the contemporary lack of locally tied police patrols. This model exhibits a more ring-fenced division of labour between CSOs and police officers.

It is important to recognise that these two models are potentially competing. A key challenge for the future of CSOs is to strike a balance between these two understandings of the CSO role. For the CSOs themselves, each model has its drawbacks. The 'junior police officer' model assumes that CSOs constitute a 'second tier of policing' within the police organisation. Unless CSOs see the job as a stepping-stone to becoming a police officer – as some clearly do – they may be affronted by the lower status accorded to their role within the hierarchy of policing.

Congested organisational demands on the police are likely to create internal pressures for police managers to use CSOs in diverse ways (for example, traffic duties at public events, crime scene guarding, house-to-house enquiries, etc). On the one hand, the deployment of CSOs to such duties might be seen as an innovative and effective use of CSOs as a resource. On the other hand, it clearly represents a degree of 'mission creep'. It is in this context that police forces need to clarify, at a strategic level, the role and responsibilities of CSOs. Otherwise, CSOs are likely to become used as a generic resource in a non-uniform manner across different divisions. This may result in the role and reception of CSOs by police officers varying between divisions, as well as significantly skewing levels of police visibility across force areas.

The 'dedicated patrol officer' model may also be problematic in that patrol alone may become viewed by CSOs as mundane, boring and repetitive, and may fail to utilise their range of skills. In this context, maintaining the enthusiasm, interest and morale of CSOs may become difficult. As such, CSOs may prefer to apply to join the ranks of sworn police officers (to develop and exploit their skills) or may leave for other careers.

For police officers, each model also has its criticisms. The 'junior police officer' model implies the notion of 'policing on the cheap'; that this new grade of police staff may be replacing fully trained sworn officers. There is a thin line between relieving officers of unwanted duties and taking away police officers' work. It evokes a 'cut-and-paste' approach to civilianisation, whereby civilian staff are drafted in to do work previously undertaken by sworn police constables.

Equally, the 'dedicated patrol officer' model may also be problematic for police officers. They may perceive that the narrow nature of the CSO role creates additional work for them; for example, in training, managing and supervising CSOs, attending incidents to support CSOs where their powers are limited to detention and acting on information provided by CSOs.

Findings from a survey of CSOs in West Yorkshire revealed high levels of job satisfaction among CSOs, with four fifths of respondents (81%) saying that they were satisfied with their job. However, it also showed that just over half (51%) disagreed that their skills were being fully used, compared with 43% who agreed (see Figure 22).

Nearly half of CSOs surveyed agreed that they could see themselves remaining in the job for the foreseeable future (48%), while a sizeable minority disagreed (34%). As Figure 22 shows, there were mixed responses as to whether the CSO role provides good career opportunities. When asked if they had plans to apply to join the police in the future, the majority of respondents (53%) replied positively as against 23% who said 'no'. A similar number said that they might consider such a career move in the future.

Figure 22: Views on skills usage and future job prospects (%)

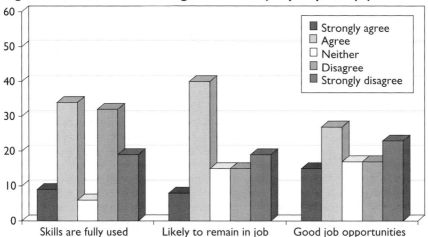

It was recognised that one of the biggest challenges is the manner in which CSOs are managed as a human resource:

> Some will come in because they want to be in the police, that's fine. The danger is that if you are a CSO on the same beat in five years' time, are you going to be happy doing that for another five years? I suspect the biggest problem we are going to have is aspiration development. (Police manager)

The problem of maintaining enthusiasm and interest in the role is captured by the following comments from a CSO who subsequently applied to become a police officer:

> It's not a mundane job because specific things happen every day. But we've got to the stage now where, unless something dramatic happens, it can run its course. You start to lose that enthusiasm because you're doing mostly the same thing day in, day out.... I always wanted to join the police anyway so it was always going to be a stepping-stone for me. I'm glad I've done it and it's taught me a lot and I'm going to hopefully get into the regulars and take a lot with me from being a CSO. But even if I hadn't have wanted to get into the regulars, I couldn't have done this for much longer.

While recruitment from CSOs into full police officers offers the police organisation significant gains, particularly in terms of recruiting from a wider range of backgrounds, it also may have adverse implications for CSOs who are not necessarily attracted to becoming a police officer:

> I'm proud of my job but I just wish they wouldn't keep recruiting people that don't actually want to be doing it. You know, recruiting the people that are just serving their time before they go into the regulars. (CSO)

Rapid staff turnover holds potentially adverse implications for the morale of those CSOs remaining in post and also, as the following quotation suggests, for the communities that they police:

> It takes you months to build up the trust of people on your beat and the contacts and everything and that's lost when somebody leaves, then somebody new comes in, you've got to start all over again. So I think you need a continuity of familiar faces to reassure people and gain valuable information from them once you've got trust. (CSO)

These comments raise questions about how to encourage long-term commitment of CSOs and whether CSOs are to be used as a recruitment and training ground for sworn police officers. If CSOs are to be more than a transient stepping-stone into the profession, consideration will need to be given to facilitating a career within the CSO role. To this end, consideration should be given to creating a supervisor grade, so that CSOs can move into more supervisory responsibilities. Many police managers interviewed during the research supported this view:

> I also think they would benefit, not to isolate them from the police force but to consolidate the fact that they are a part of the police force with a structure of some kind that will allow progression. (Police sergeant)

The police service faces a large cultural challenge to integrate CSOs into the wider police service, not as a separate sub-organisation within the police, akin to traffic wardens. There has been a tendency to treat sworn officers and police staff in separate silos as if they were not part of the same organisation. A more integrated approach to police professionalism needs to be developed. Some time ago, the Audit Commission noted the cultural and institutional barriers that serve to ghettoise traffic wardens and other civilian staff:

> The low status of traffic wardens inside the police service is partly a reflection of the barriers in the service between 'real' police officers, who can exercise the power of constable and who carry warrant cards to prove it, and civilian support. This barrier needs to be broken down. (Audit Commission, 1992, p 21)

The recent thematic report on workforce modernisation from Her Majesty's Inspectorate of Constabulary (HMIC, 2004) highlights this challenge and has a number of important recommendations with regard to the modernisation of the police workforce, some (but not all) of which the government has decided to pursue in its *Building communities, beating crime* White Paper (Home Office, 2004d, Chapter 4).

At different levels of the organisation, police forces need to confront the often unintended signals sent out that police staff such as CSOs are less valued or less capable than sworn police officers. There is a need to move away from the current twin-track approach to the recruitment, training, progression and management of civilian staff. This would see the development of more structured and flexible career pathways for CSOs, opening up the possibility of a more integrated career structure with opportunities for 'crossover points'. There is a need to develop clear career pathways for CSOs both within the role and within the wider police organisation. Similarly, clearer career paths within and between police officers and civilian staff, warden schemes and private security should be mapped out, allowing for different points of entry and transfer of skills.

Wardens and reassurance

Only two fifths of residents surveyed said that they were aware that neighbourhood wardens worked in the Halton Moor area, despite the fact that wardens had been working in the area for more than two years since early 2002. By comparison, less than one fifth were aware of the private security patrols in the area. Just over half had never seen a warden. Older people were slightly more likely to say that they had never seen a warden, which may be explained by the fact that they tend to spend less time out in public places within the estate.

Only 14% of Halton Moor residents surveyed said that they knew the name of the neighbourhood warden and less than one in 10 said that they were aware of the warden Freephone number. Less than 2% had ever used the Freephone service. By contrast, some 39% of respondents said that they had phoned the local police in the previous two years either for an emergency or non-emergency (half had done so more than once). In interviews, a number of residents commented on problems experienced in trying to use the Freephone service. They reported that it was not in operation late in the evening and that in most cases if an incident was serious they were advised to call the police.

By comparison, more than two thirds of residents surveyed in Foxwood were aware that community rangers provided by a private security company patrolled the area. Most of those who were aware of the patrols had seen them in operation. However, two fifths had never seen a community ranger, while nearly a fifth of residents said they saw rangers at least once a week. Only two respondents (less than 0.4%) said that they knew any of the rangers by name and only 15% said they were aware of the rangers' Freephone number. Only 3% had ever used the Freephone service. Nearly half said that they had phoned the local police in the previous two years, either for an emergency or non-emergency (more than half had done so more than once).

The impact of the decline in overall recorded crime in Halton Moor, by 7% in 2002-03 and 1% in 2003-04 on the previous year (see Figure 11, p 26), would appear to be appreciated by local people. Significantly more residents on the Halton Moor estate said that they felt the level of crime had decreased over the preceding two years (37%: 27% saying 'a little less' and 10% saying 'a lot less'), as against 24% who believed crime had increased (14% saying 'a lot more' and 10% saying 'a little more') and 31% who said crime had remained much the same. This contrasts quite starkly with national findings from the British Crime Survey over the same period. This shows that when asked about crime in their local area, nearly half (48%) of the public thought that local crime had increased, with one in five (20%) believing that it had increased 'a lot' (Dodd et al, 2004, p 17).

In both the residential areas, respondents were asked about the extent to which the visible presence of different patrol officers served to reassure them as to their personal safety. Figure 23 shows that in Halton Moor, unsurprisingly, the police are the most reassuring. It also suggests that private security officers are seen as reassuring by more people than neighbourhood wardens; 38% said that the private security officers were at least 'a little' reassuring, as against 28% who said this about neighbourhood wardens. This is partly explained by the lower level of visibility of wardens, patrol being a limited part of their work. However, more people thought that neighbourhood wardens were important to the overall level of policing in Halton Moor (40%) compared with private security patrols (32%). Some 35% of respondents felt safer during the day as a result of the neighbourhood wardens, as against 24% who said they felt safer in the evenings as a result of the private security patrols. The survey revealed that a significant proportion of the local population was unable to judge the value of different patrol personnel, because they were unaware of the presence on the estate of such officers.

Figure 23: Reassurance value of different patrol personnel in Halton Moor (%)

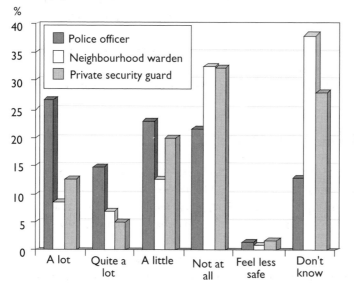

Figure 24: Reassurance value of different patrol personnel in Foxwood (%)

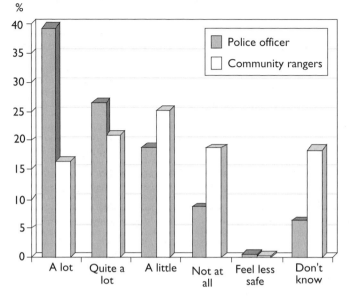

Nearly a third of respondents (32%) had confidence in the neighbourhood wardens to cope with low-level crime and anti-social behaviour in Halton Moor, compared with 39% who did not. A slightly lower number (27%) had confidence in the private security patrols as against 34% who did not have such confidence.

In Foxwood, as in Halton Moor, police officers were seen as most reassuring (Figure 24). However, community rangers were seen as at least 'a little' reassuring by 63% of people. Nearly half thought that community rangers were important to the overall level of policing in Foxwood and some 28% said that they felt safer during the day and 31% safer at night as a result of the community rangers' patrols.

Nearly a third of respondents said that they had confidence in the community rangers to cope with low-level crime and anti-social behaviour in Foxwood, whereas a similar but slightly larger number did not have much confidence.

Private security and reassurance

Across three surveys of visitors to the MetroCentre[3], an average of 94% of respondents said that security was important for their shopping or leisure experience (see Figure 25). Of the total, 80% said it was very important. By contrast, less than 4% of respondents said that feeling secure was not very or not

---

[3] Visitor surveys were conducted at three different times: pre-Christmas 'peak' survey (December 2002); summer 'off-peak' survey (August 2003); and pre-Christmas 'peak' survey (December 2003). On each occasion, approximately 500 surveys were completed, representing an overall sample of just under 1,500.

Figure 25: Importance of feeling secure in the MetroCentre (%)

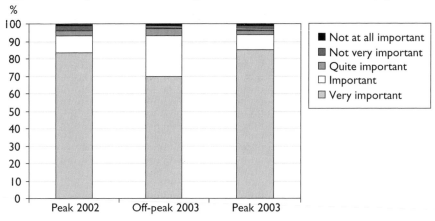

at all important. Figure 25 shows that 'peak time' shoppers were more likely to identify security as very important and that there is no significant shift in attitudes to security between 2002 and 2003.

Respondents were also asked how safe and secure they felt visiting the MetroCentre, compared with other shopping and leisure environments (Figure 26). Across all three surveys, an average of 72% of respondents said that they felt safer in the MetroCentre than in comparable shopping or leisure centres. Of the total, 43% said they felt much safer. Only just over 1% felt less safe, when aggregated across all three surveys. There was no discernable change in views on relative safety between 2002 and 2003.

Figure 26: Comparative feelings of safety in the MetroCentre as against other outlets (%)

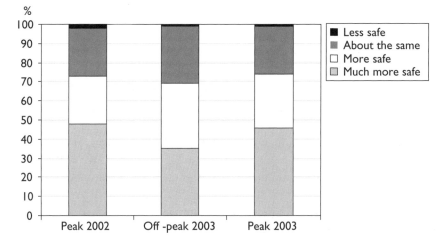

In order to assess the level of visibility of security personnel, visitors were asked whether they had seen either a police officer or a MetroCentre security guard during their visit. According to survey data, the average length of visits to the MetroCentre is approximately two and a half hours[4].

Figure 27: Visibility of police and security guards during visit (%)

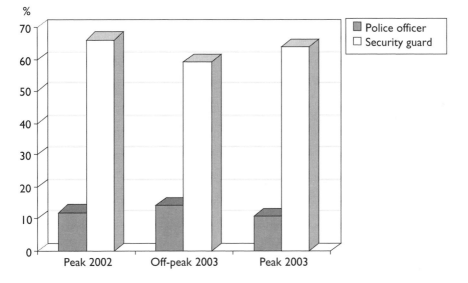

Across the three surveys, an average of 12% of visitors saw a police officer during their visit to the MetroCentre. This compares with 63% of visitors who saw a security guard. In terms of visible reassurance, security guards play a dominant role in the MetroCentre (see Figure 27). Again there is no discernable trend over time, except for the observation that during the 'off peak' survey period respondents were more likely to have seen a police officer and less likely to have seen a security guard compared with 'peak' time respondents. Consequently, less than a third of visitors said that they saw neither a police officer nor a security guard during their visit.

Public reception and identity

For many members of the public, the confidence and reassurance vested in CSOs is enhanced by their uniform and police identity. Despite their limited powers, CSOs are perceived to be reassuring, in large part because members of the public often assume that they have received appropriate vetting and training and, importantly, can summon rapid support from police officer colleagues. While many members of the public invest considerable symbolic prestige and emotional attachment to the

---

[4] The survey data show that the average 'spend productivity' (ie capita spent per minute) was 50p in 2002, up from 28p in 1998.

police, their cultural image and 'sacred' character, business people and individual citizens also adopt instrumental approaches to policing, notably with regard both to cost and effectiveness.

> I would not agree to pay any more taxes for policing, as that is what my existing taxes go toward. I have worked all my life and don't see why I should pay extra, but would not mind contributing to a private security scheme if it was proved to work. (Halton Moor resident)

Comparative experiences from other European countries, particularly where there is more extensive regulation, suggest that the policing division of labour in the field of reassurance patrols in the UK is poorly organised and subject to considerable local variation, and that the demarcation of roles and responsibilities is inadequately coordinated. A blurring of roles and uncertain differentiation of identity create significant public confusion about the variety of forms of visible policing and types of uniform as well as their powers and limitations.

Focus group interviews and surveys in the different sites reveal that members of the public are unclear as to the responsibilities of different officers, their levels of training and the nature of their powers. Yet, these factors are seen as important in providing reassurance, particularly with regard to CSOs. Moreover, the limitations of the different roles were not clearly understood. As a consequence, for example, members of the public often assume that CSOs can act like sworn police officers – reinforced by the fact that they have the word 'Police' in large letters across their uniforms. This suggests that false expectations may arise among the public over precisely what CSOs can legitimately do.

The challenge of coordination

The case studies in our research, as examples of well-coordinated security partnerships, are largely atypical of developments elsewhere. Nevertheless, they highlight the difficulties in establishing and maintaining well-coordinated security networks incorporating plural providers, even where the explicit desire to do so exists. The research highlights that in many areas plural policing providers pass each other like 'ships in the night'. In some instances, as in the Trafford Park Industrial Estate, the sheer diversity of private security firms presents acute coordination problems. The autonomy of the market can foster fragmentation of service delivery.

The short-term nature of many contracts for additional policing and of government funding initiatives engenders a piecemeal approach to the mixed economy. This generates significant turnover and flux in the delivery of community safety. Furthermore, it often serves to undermine the development of strong bonds between policing personnel and local communities as funding shifts, providers are replaced and the priorities of initiatives change.

Organising the division of labour and coordination

Coordination is best ensured if it is delivered at a number of mutually reinforcing and supportive levels:

- joined-up national government initiatives, policies and legislation;
- regional oversight;
- strategic coordination and partnership; and
- operational coordination.

Coordination deficits are not only a product of the nature of local relations between different plural policing providers, but are also structured by central government's lack of genuine joined-up thinking. In recent years, there have been significant coordination deficits at the level of national policy. This has been particularly evident over the role of wardens and the relationship between wardens, community support officers (CSOs), accreditation schemes and the regulation of private security:

> The mixed economy has been a reality in policing for some time, it's just it hasn't quite been joined up and still isn't because of rivalries and turf wars, as much

between government ministries as anything else.... What do we want to achieve? Or are we just going to end up with dozens of different uniforms, you know, purple, green, red, yellow, blue, etc out there, the public utterly confused and no sense of synergy, no sense of joint working or tasking? You can get more out of all these people than the simple sum of their parts if you coordinate it properly. (Chief Constable)

Government needs to reflect on whether new initiatives and policies encourage conditions that foster and sustain joint partnerships and collaborative local action.

Many providers of plural policing do not have organisational boundaries coterminous with police forces. Hence, regional oversight can provide important cross-force coordination and standard setting, and promote best practice (to which we return in Chapter 6).

Strategic coordination and partnership

Cooperation through close partnership working across forms of plural policing will often require considerable effort in time and resources from the police. Such efforts are too often tied to individual officers, the subsequent movement of whom can undermine any momentum that has developed towards effective partnership working. Hence, strategic-level policy may be required to sustain and clarify the nature and extent of joint working practices.

Force-wide police units can be useful in organising and coordinating efforts within the extended policing family, and in providing strategic oversight, such as the West Yorkshire Plural Policing Unit:

> This unit has been formed in recognition of the fact that many policing services can be delivered by non-sworn officers and that many individuals and organisations have a huge contribution to make in helping to create safer societies ... The unit will serve as a focal point to help in the process of joined-up working between police officers and those members of what we now term as 'the extended police family' to ensure that we deliver the best possible quality of service to our communities. (Chief Superintendent)

Strategic units such as this are well placed to:

- coordinate community safety accreditation schemes;
- work with special constables, particularly to avoid any problems of specials being marginalised or undervalued by a focus on CSOs;
- work with traffic wardens to avoid uncertainties over the warden role;
- help to manage broader developments in civilianisation within the police organisation;

- work with the 'extended police family' beyond the police organisation;
- engage with the private security industry; and
- work with the SIA as it implements the new occupational licensing regime.

A well-coordinated division of labour produces benefits in terms of information exchange, familiarity and trust. Practical means of achieving better strategic-level coordination include:

- Structured briefings and regular partnership meetings of diverse providers at strategic levels.
- The establishment of information-sharing protocols between the plural policing providers, notably the police and private security, but also municipal policing personnel.

Involvement and links with local crime and disorder reduction partnerships (CDRPs) as a channel through which to foster coordination, improve information exchange and forge a degree of local accountability.

CDRPs are an important local vehicle in assisting coordination and providing a degree of local oversight. To do so, these partnerships, which remain dominated by the public sector, need to engage more actively than at present with commercial policing providers and the private sector more generally. In addition, the current dominant position of the police within CDRPs needs to be addressed if they are to provide robust independent oversight.

Operational coordination

Central to the delivery of operational coordination is the dedication of patrol personnel to specific geographic areas or sectors. Where they are localised to small areas, individual patrol personnel can build up trust relations with local communities, residents, businesses and visitors. Coterminous boundaries of plural policing personnel and organisations will facilitate coordination. Personnel that are dedicated to specific geographic areas or sectors – such as the MetroCentre community beat managers (CBMs), the Gold Zones teams in Liverpool and neighbourhood wardens in Halton Moor – can develop close relationships with their local communities and get to know the policing issues and problems in the area. It allows patrol personnel to tailor their strategies to the needs of the locality – for example, different Gold Zones developed somewhat different policing priorities, reflecting the demands of divergent areas.

CSOs offer a key resource through which to operationalise and support the concept of the 'extended police family', allowing the police to enhance community safety by harnessing the diverse work of other security personnel. However, it requires the police to learn better to manage, steer and coordinate the policing efforts of others. There remains considerably greater scope to work with street and neighbourhood wardens, private security personnel, traffic wardens and parking attendants. To do so, the police service must continue to challenge the view that persists among some officers that they alone should provide visible patrols, rather than seeing the policing efforts of others as a resource to be harnessed in the furtherance of public safety. To this end, CSOs constitute an important street-level link in the chain that binds together the diverse service providers that impact, directly and indirectly, on crime and disorder.

Geographically based, integrated teams that draw together personnel from different policing organisations can afford:

- a clearer division of labour and organisation of the respective roles and responsibilities of the partners, reducing duplication and conflict;
- better understanding of the limitations of the different partner organisations and personnel;
- clearer mutual expectations for the different organisations and individuals who work as visible patrol personnel;
- enhanced and stable inter-personal and inter-organisational relations of trust and confidence; and
- improved information exchange between the parties.

Models of local policing teams

The government's commitment in the *Building communities, beating crime* White Paper (Home Office, 2004d) to implement the spread of dedicated neighbourhood policing teams across the country is to be welcomed. However, careful consideration should be given to the different models of policing teams and their appropriateness for different communities. The following models were identified by the research:

Linked policing teams: Here, plural policing personnel work alongside each other within dedicated geographic areas, liaising with regard to information exchange but not subject to joint tasking or integrated supervision and management. Deployment and control rests with the managerial structures of the different agencies. Such teams benefit from strategic-level agreements and regular meetings to review policing priorities and tactics. Here, coordination rather than co-production is the primary purpose of teams. The MetroCentre's links between Northumbria Police and the centre's security staff and management are a good example of the advantages derived from this model of coordinated delivery.

MetroCentre

The MetroCentre is geographically divided into four malls together with the service yards and the car parks. The eight contracted police constables, CBMs from Northumbria Police, are each dedicated to a specific mall to provide visible patrols (two CBMs per mall). They work closely with centre management, St James' Security (the centre's security contractors) and in-store security guards, holding monthly tasking and coordination meetings. CBMs work from a police station located within the centre and are managed by a dedicated sergeant. During opening hours, there are at least four St James' security guards on each mall at any one time. Information protocols structure data exchange.

Police-organised integrated police teams: These teams incorporate police officers and police staff dedicated to specific local policing areas under the supervision and control of a police manager. As a model, it ensures that the work of CSOs, while distinct from that of police constables, is integrated into the work of the wider police organisation through local teams. It also ensures that there is no binary divide between CSOs performing visible non-confrontational roles while police constables are restricted to reactive and often confrontational interactions with the public. This model could be extended to include dedicated special constables as well as citizen volunteers.

Safer neighbourhoods teams

The Metropolitan Police's safer neighbourhoods teams, in each of London's 32 boroughs, combine a sergeant, two constables and three CSOs, dedicated to a local area. Their role is to work with the community and local authorities to reduce crime and disorder and deal with the local issues that most affect people's quality of life.

Police-organised extended policing teams: Here, teams incorporate plural policing personnel beyond the 'immediate police family', such as street or neighbourhood wardens, parks police or other security and environment officers, dedicated to specific local policing areas under the supervision and control of a police manager. The Bradford city centre teams of street wardens and CSOs supervised by a police sergeant are a good example of this model of deployment. Similarly, the Barnsley local partnership teams (LPTs, see p 74) provide an indication of the range of personnel that can be incorporated within such teams. They might also seek, where relevant, to incorporate or work closely with other policing personnel, such as private security where community safety accreditation schemes are in place.

Bradford City Centre policing team

Bradford South has a dedicated city centre team managed by a police
inspector. The team consists of a divisional patrol unit (two sergeants and
12 constables), two dedicated city centre beat constables, a 'retail theft'
constable, and 30 CSOs supervised by two police sergeants. In addition, 14
traffic wardens are attached to the team with two traffic warden supervisors.
Working in partnership with the city centre team are 14 Bradford Council
street wardens with their own supervisors, administration support and
management. The street wardens operate out of the same police station and
are jointly deployed.

Local authority-organised extended policing teams: In this model, plural policing
personnel are integrated into a team managed or tasked by council officers outside
of police employment. The Barnsley LPTs are innovative not only in the breadth of
personnel incorporated within the teams, but also for the fact that 'tasking officers'
are council employees. LPTs usually consist of a tasking officer, police sergeant,
CSO supervisor, 'impact warden' supervisor, seven police constables, one school
liaison constable, six CSOs and three 'impact wardens' working together from one
location with a focused approach to addressing quality-of-life issues. The role of
council-employed tasking officers raises issues regarding operational control over
police resources and questions concerning access to confidential police information.
In Barnsley, the police team supervisor retains operational control over CSOs in
consultation with the tasking officer. In the absence of a police team supervisor,
the tasking officer can only deploy CSOs after consultation with the duty inspector
or chief inspector of operations. Furthermore, police concerns regarding the lack
of managerial and disciplinary control over the tasking officer are addressed by
changing the council disciplinary regulation so that individuals can be appropriately
disciplined for improper use of confidential police information. The Barnsley LPTs
are good examples of the potential for such innovative arrangements. More
radically, again, teams might also seek to incorporate other policing personnel, such
as private security, where community safety accreditation schemes are in place.

Barnsley's local partnership teams

The LPTs and Neighbourhood Safety Units are multi-agency teams resourced
by Barnsley Metropolitan Borough Council, South Yorkshire Police and the
CDRP. LPTs have been established by merging specially trained staff who are
not police officers into existing police units. In total, there are five LPTs made
up of 45 police officers, 28 CSOs, 23 special constables, four tasking officers, 16
impact wardens, four anti-social behaviour managers, four community service
desk staff, one community cohesion tactical analyst, one solicitor and four
community service facilitators. A key element in this initiative was the decision

by Barnsley Metropolitan District Council to fund 21 CSOs for three years at an approximate cost of £2.7 million. Tasking officers are council employees with access to police data, who task CSOs and warden supervisors.

In its White Paper *Building communities, beating crime* (Home Office, 2004d), the government appears to have opted for the Metropolitan Police's model of neighbourhood policing teams, but careful consideration should be given to some of the other, more expansive, models that offer coordination and community safety benefits beyond those restricted to the police. In addition, community safety accreditation schemes afford a significant opportunity for the police and private security industry to engage in more productive relations and enhance cooperation.

However, it will often be in the interests of the police and local authorities to limit the number of plural policing providers with which they have to work in the name of coordination, notably in their interactions with the private sector. For example, an implicit perceived benefit of the Guardsafe scheme in Trafford Park was a reduction in the number of different private sector providers working on the industrial estate. Furthermore, the coordination and managerial oversight of private security patrols by Safer York Partnership has similarly fostered a less differentiated market. While coordination is facilitated by standardisation and uniformity of approach, this can fly in the face of local autonomy and choice over security provider and undermine the market by fostering consolidation and monopolistic tendencies. In York, council officers wished to instigate a 'city-wide single provider' contract for a residential patrol service. Such formal streamlining of service provision aimed to facilitate oversight and coordination endeavours. However, on the grounds of local democracy and accountability, council members resisted such an approach to procurement. They insisted that highly localised structures of governance (that is, ward committees) must retain the right to opt in or out of the patrol service, as well the right to choose their local patrol provider.

Information exchange

Confident and effective information exchange is central to policing partnerships. Information exchange relies on, and also reinforces, good relations between partners, and especially mutual trust. The effectiveness of information exchange arrangements is a reflection of the effectiveness of partnerships as a whole.

Section 115 of the 1998 Crime and Disorder Act facilitates considerable information exchange among key public authorities. However, the implications of this power have still not filtered into all areas of local delivery of CDRPs. Furthermore, section 115 also covers disclosure to people acting on behalf of the responsible authorities of CDRPs, the implications of which again have been little exploited. Concerns over confidentiality and data protection often thwart close partnership cooperation.

Police sometimes invoke data protection as a reason for non-engagement with partnerships (as do others, most notably probation and health services). However, some concerns are often based on poor understanding or misinterpretations of the data protection regime and the powers to disclose information under the 1998 Act.

Good practice often results in the exchange of high-quality aggregated crime information, as the data protection regime does not affect the disclosure of information that has been 'aggregated up' so that individual people are not identifiable. Nevertheless, this information can be very useful in the deployment and targeting of patrol and security resources by different plural policing organisations. On the basis of this kind of aggregated data, crime and disorder trends, patterns and hot spots can be analysed and displayed by local area.

Where effective partnerships exist, the exchange of personalised information is frequently governed by predetermined protocols identifying where disclosure is strictly justified. Data protection requires that personal data are obtained and processed fairly and lawfully; are only disclosed in appropriate circumstances; are accurate, relevant, and not held longer than necessary; and are kept securely. Operating within carefully prepared information-sharing protocols between organisations will often be the best way of ensuring that disclosure is appropriately handled.

The Bichard Inquiry Report exposed serious failures in police recording and managing information. These failures were not merely 'systemic and corporate' but 'endemic' and include local systems for recording, retaining and accessing data. The report identified a "widespread failure to appreciate the value of intelligence" and shortcomings that suggest "that the importance everyone concerned professes to give intelligence was not borne out in reality" (Bichard, 2004, p 5).

Our research suggests that the rigorous collation, analysis and use of community intelligence gathered by patrol personnel remains the exception rather than the norm. In part, this is due to the large volume and the low-level nature of the intelligence, but is also a product of the significant cultural and organisational obstacles surrounding police information gathering, analysis and exchange and the institutionalisation of intelligence-led policing (Cope, 2004).

Community intelligence and local information generated by neighbourhood wardens and private security patrols is often poorly used by the police. The collection, analysis and dissemination of information tend to be ad hoc and informal. There was little linkage between community intelligence, reassurance activities and police National Intelligence Model (NIM) integration[1]. In many instances,

---

[1] NIM is a formula, developed by the National Criminal Intelligence Service (NCIS), for coordinating the gathering, dissemination and use of intelligence. Its assessment procedures provide data for policing prirorities to be set.

information 'passed on' to the police is disregarded or ignored unless it relates or may be of some use in relation to an incident brought to the police's attention. In part, this is due to the large volume and poor quality of some of the information gathered. For example, private security firms routinely hand over to the police visual tape recordings of their mobile patrols (as was the case in Foxwood). It may be difficult to know how such information is of use to the police. This stems from a lack of clarity on both sides as to what information might be of use and the form in which this information should be provided and organised.

Where local policing teams work within dedicated structures, an informal approach to information exchange is less problematic as intelligence is more likely to be shared among team members. Nevertheless, it is important that community intelligence feeds into wider operational activities and the NIM. Police forces need to develop a more systematic and structured approach to community intelligence collection, storage and use. This raises particular questions surrounding the role of CSOs and wardens as gatherers of community-level information and intelligence. Unless there are the appropriate support structures and personnel in place, this information gathering is likely to be of little use beyond the individual officers and their immediate colleagues.

Bradford policing teams

In Bradford, the deployment of CSOs, combined with the introduction of the NIM, required the police to recruit two extra crime analysts to input on to the police database the extra intelligence generated. The CSOs alone produced approximately 120 intelligence forms per week. Without these additional staff, it is doubtful that the police would have been able to cope in any meaningful sense with the volume of intelligence generated by CSOs. The data were used to target deployment and resource allocation.

In the residential sites in the research there was little systematic use of intelligence gathered by private security firms or even neighbourhood wardens, unless the information was explicitly sought by the police or local authority. Nevertheless, the local information gathered by non-police patrol personnel, particularly where they benefit from highly developed local knowledge, can be of significant use in community policing, problem solving and crime prevention endeavours. It can facilitate intelligence-led patrolling that deploys the most up-to-date information, effectively targeting criminal behaviour, anti-social conduct and insecurity hot spots.

In mature partnerships, information exchange is not a one-way process from police to private security, as implied by some commentators (Ericson and Haggerty, 1997). Police increasingly come to rely on information provided by private security and other plural policing bodies. The local intelligence gathered and collected by private security in shopping and commercial centres such as Liverpool Gold Zones and the MetroCentre can be highly sophisticated. Where police appreciate the value of such information exchange and sharing, there can be mutual benefits for the different partners.

> **Information exchange in the MetroCentre**
>
> The MetroCentre Information System (MIS) holds photographs and information on offenders (that is, the type of offence they are associated with and their modus operandi). Senior members of St James' Security, the X-ray team and the police have access to this database. There is also a 'target file' of offenders, suspects, exclusions and those who have been 'deterred', which is available for all St James' staff and police. The database can be used for analysing patterns, profiles and 'hot spots'. As some victims contact the police directly, the information on the database is updated regularly with police-provided information. The database includes 'deterrence' files, where an individual has been stopped from committing a crime but the police were not involved. In these instances, security staff contact the CCTV control room and capture images of the offender, collating them on a 'deterrence database'. If the person offends again, security can check their details and verify whether they are a 'repeat offender' necessitating police action. The MIS also holds records on all people who are excluded from the MetroCentre. Information from the MIS is circulated at the weekly Crime and Disorder Watch meetings.

The provision of additional security as a 'club good'

Plural policing partnerships encourage 'clubbing' endeavours, whereby individual private concerns club together to provide collective security needs. Club goods, such as additional visible policing and security, are those 'quasi-public' goods that are available to members of a club but restricted in some form or other to non-members. Such clubbing endeavours are often stymied by the problem of 'free-riders'. Individuals or businesses may prefer to benefit from a service without paying for it. As the 'prisoner's dilemma' reminds us, each person, household or business has an incentive not to cooperate, even though all would gain more if all cooperated. However, this ignores the various incentives to cooperation (or disincentives not to cooperate) that may exist, rooted more in social, rather than economic, capital. The process of clubbing may entail using diverse levers to encourage 'consensual' cooperation, where a narrow economic interpretation of self-interest may suggest otherwise.

Club formation can also be facilitated and undermined by membership size, spatial landscape, architecture and environmental design, as well as the existence of some collective authority that can encourage, induce or coerce compliance and raise costs, such as the MetroCentre management or a local authority-devolved committee with budgetary powers. Funding may arise through rent, fees, service charges or government sources (ultimately through taxation). The various research sites witnessed several attempts to motivate collective endeavours against crime, disorder and insecurity.

On the Trafford Park Industrial Estate, a number of attempts to encourage clubbing were fostered through the government-funded policing initiative, albeit not always successfully. As a result of high crime within the business park in the late 1990s, concerns were raised about businesses relocating to potentially safer locations. To counteract the threat of theft and other crime, most individual businesses employed separate and often disparate private security firms, with cost often being the determining factor. As a consequence, the business park was policed by a plethora of security firms with little collective coordination. This in turn introduced new security concerns over the extent to which some security provision within the park was either exposed to organised criminality or seen as insufficiently robust. While it was in the interests of all businesses to render the site more secure, high transaction costs were associated with this objective. A variety of initiatives were introduced that illustrate some of the difficulties of clubbing:

First, the industrial estate's large size did not help. With the support of the council, road closures and environmental planning changes were implemented to encourage smaller subunits that might club together. Here, the ambition was to facilitate clusters of businesses to implement greater situational crime controls, as well as purchase manned security from fewer, if not a single supplier.

Second, a Guardsafe scheme was introduced with the support of the local police to try to standardise the quality of private security through limited training and introduce a form of regulation. In so doing, the aim was to facilitate closer working practices between public and private policing agencies, notably through more regular and formal processes of information exchange.

Third, Business Watch, the collective voice of businesses within the park, worked with the local police to coordinate security provision and sought to provide additional policing through a variety of funding sources.

Finally, the police encouraged businesses to form crime risk management groups in an attempt to familiarise themselves with their 'shared' risks or experiences of victimisation and, hence, to seek collective solutions.

None of the above strategies fully addressed all the problems of clubbing in the area. Trafford Park remained policed by fragmented private security and many businesses preferred not to become members of Business Watch or participate in its activities. Police identified absentee landlords – that is, businesses owned by pension funds and foreign investment portfolios – on the estate as contributing to the difficulties associated with clubbing.

The short-term nature of much government funding and the precarious nature of the market (short-term contracts) were identified as features hindering clubbing endeavours. Uncertainties over the renewal of security contracts were highlighted as key reasons for security companies' unwillingness to invest in Guardsafe training for their staff on the Trafford Park Industrial Estate, demonstrating again how economic imperatives can undermine coordination efforts.

Information exchange and access to communication systems can be promoted as one way of encouraging clubbing, for example, access to radio or CCTV systems or crime-related information. In the Liverpool Gold Zones, the Business Crime Direct radio-alert link (see Chapter 3) acted as a mechanism through which to draw individual businesses together and forge collective security interests. In the two-year period from March 2002, some 1,003 incidents and 773 offenders were entered onto the Business Information Crime System database. Information is supplied by stores that are members of the Business Crime Direct scheme. Photograph albums of persistent offenders involved in shop theft and other crimes relating to the city centre are circulated to the businesses involved in the scheme. Consequently, shared databases, such as the MetroCentre MIS holding information on offenders and suspects are often collective resources that can be contributed to and drawn on by club members.

In many of these parochial initiatives the police are able to, and do, act as key 'honest brokers', helping to facilitate 'club' formation. Here, the police act in a steering capacity, facilitating and stimulating the collective action of others.

Questions of governance and accountability

6

The contemporary mixed economy of visible patrols and the pluralisation of policing demand robust forms of governance, regulation and accountability that are fit for the tasks required of them. In the conclusion to its Discussion Paper, the Law Commission of Canada posed the following crucial question:

> What are the best governance mechanisms to ensure that policing is delivered in accordance with the democratic values of justice, equality, accountability and efficiency? (Law Commission of Canada, 2002, p 56)

Demands for security, given their subjective nature and future orientation, are not always in keeping with concerns for justice. Private security strategies and social justice are not necessarily congruent, though neither are they mutually exclusive. Moreover, the growing market for additional security and policing has produced an unequal distribution. While some areas have a surfeit of policing and security, others experience a policing deficit. Access to enhanced security (often through the market) is primarily determined by wealth as well as the financial and organisational capacity of groups and businesses to club together to purchase additional security. This raises concerns that policing may become greater in affluent areas, where people have the loudest voices, the largest political influence and the deepest pockets. One of the central paradoxes of crime prevention and security is found in the often inverse relationship between activity and need (Crawford, 1998), and hence, security tends not to be concentrated where most needed.

The inequitable distribution of policing in favour of affluent areas challenges (both central and local) governments to think creatively about how to respond to the security deficit experienced in some of the poorer parts of the country. Targeted regeneration funding and the provision of neighbourhood wardens have been important responses to this problem. A more radical solution is the provision of 'block grants' or 'security budgets' to disadvantaged communities enabling them to purchase additional security, whether from the police or other providers (Shearing, 2000).

Our research shows that, increasingly, local authorities are devolving certain budgets to neighbourhood committee structures, often including a community safety or security element, thus giving local people a greater say over how additional security is to be provided. In York, for example, ward-level devolved council budgets have been used to fund private security patrols. In Leeds, by contrast, each of the 11 area committees that make up the city have a 'well-being' budget that is linked to council priorities, but with flexibility for local discretion. These committees have voted on whether they wish to continue to fund neighbourhood wardens through these budgets or to spend the money contributing to community support officers (CSOs). As a consequence, during 2004, Leeds City Council has had to reduce by 19 the number of warden posts across the city as significant numbers of area committees opted to use their budgetary powers to fund CSOs.

'Security budgets' invest a novel degree of local ownership over the purchased policing resource. They potentially allow for a re-engagement on the part of communities with locally based policing processes. In residential areas, experiences suggest that contracted additional security patrols also:

- raise expectations over the nature and quality of service provision;
- raise demands for greater accountability for the service provided, including reports on activities and results;
- raise expectations regarding responsiveness to incidents and residents' concerns; and
- give residents a greater investment and stake in local policing endeavours and their contribution (Crawford and Lister, 2004).

However, security budgets can introduce further competitive tendencies between providers as they vie for limited funding. They can produce coordination difficulties, notably where areas opt for different providers. Moreover, the short-term nature of such arrangements, which are frequently fixed into annual financial cycles, can exacerbate this. The introduction of security budgets is likely to serve to entrench and bolster the market for security and patrol. It might increase choice, but simultaneously present significant problems for coordination. Security budgets that target resources at high-crime and disadvantaged neighbourhoods may be less politically acceptable. Affluent taxpayers might conclude that they are paying three times for security: first, by way of taxes to support the public police; second, through the expense of hiring private security; and third, through additional taxes to subsidise the entry of the poor into the commercial security market.

Nevertheless, it is conceivable that the public police will not be able to compensate fully for the lack of community-based policing (rather than reactive policing) in poorer areas as access to the market for additional security favours the affluent. This inequity in distribution of security challenges governments to ensure that visible security does not become a defining attribute of social differentiation.

Challenges to governance and accountability

The research highlights a number of key governance and accountability challenges raised by the pluralisation of policing and the mixed economy of patrol.

Accountability and 'the problem of many hands' in policing networks

Additional policing patrols are often the product of complex partnerships that tie diverse organisations together in a corporate approach to crime reduction and public reassurance. As such, they often cut across and transcend intra-organisational lines of accountability. Such partnerships may exist outside of traditional hierarchies of control, often entailing multiple layers of authority and complex relations of interdependency. Joint and negotiated decisions tie the various parties into collective agendas to which individual partners may not be directly responsible. Institutional complexity further obscures who is accountable to whom and for what. This gives rise to what Rhodes has identified as "'the problem of many hands' where so many people contribute that no one contribution can be identified; and if no one person can be held accountable after the event, then no one needs to behave responsibly beforehand" (1996, p 663). In complex networks where authority is 'shared', the various tiers of responsibility become difficult to disentangle and can become almost elusive. Networks are less transparent, hence the need to specify lines of responsibility.

Compartmentalised and segmented regulation

In contrast to the increasingly fluid, plural and networked nature of policing provision, regulation is highly segmented and compartmentalised. Different forms of patrol are (or will be) the subject of different regulatory regimes. The commercial security industry has a new regulatory body, the Security Industry Authority (SIA), and the police now have a new independent authority for managing complaints, namely the Independent Police Complaints Commission (IPCC). However, other forms of policing are regulated and governed differently. While the IPCC will manage complaints with regard to those employed by the police, neighbourhood wardens and private security fall outside of their remit. The relative robustness of different regulatory regimes is an issue of policy concern.

Police as competitor and accreditor

The current makeup of the mixed economy places the police in an ambiguous position of accreditor and competitor, raising potential conflicts of interests. Should the police regulate and accredit the policing activities of others, while simultaneously competing with those other providers? Chief police officers may find themselves in the invidious position of deciding whether to award a competitive advantage to private security companies or neighbourhood wardens – through police accreditation – while at the same time attempting to sell additional police, CSO or special constable patrols to precisely the same purchasers as those of their competitors. As local authorities consider how to spend their resources in the light of the termination of government funding for neighbourhood wardens, the relative attraction of funding either a police officer, private security guard or a warden through mainstream budgets may depend on the willingness of the police to cooperate with different plural policing providers. It may not be in the police interest to foster too close a relationship with competitors, particularly as many police forces have accepted the carrot of initial Home Office funding for CSOs without necessarily knowing how these will be funded in the long term. In an increasingly competitive marketplace, these pressures may encourage counter-productive relations between different plural policing providers, in which the police relationship may be coloured by the nature of their competitive market relation rather than the quality of policing or its capacity to serve the public good.

To this end, it may be necessary to introduce an 'honest broker' above and outside of competing interests to ensure appropriate standards, promote effective joint working and safeguard the public interest in the form of regional and local policing boards (Loader, 2000). The purpose of such boards would be to provide crucial oversight, cross-cutting the segmented regulatory bodies to formulate policies and coordinate service delivery across plural policing providers (to which we return below).

Public accountability of private and parochial initiatives

As well as parochial forms of accountability to local beneficiaries of patrol services, private or locally tied additional policing and security arrangements raise wider public implications, for which few mechanisms of accountability currently exist. Most obviously, local additional patrols may serve to displace crime and anti-social behaviour to neighbouring areas, or at least may increase the fear of crime in surrounding localities, particularly where they are not the recipients of additional forms of policing. Local initiatives can raise important implications for the wider public sphere and introduce other accountability audiences beyond the confines of those immediate parties to a contractual arrangement. These external audiences invariably do not have a voice in, nor are privy to, any local contractual mechanisms of accountability, requiring wider forms of accountability and governance. This prompts the question: how can the activities and endeavours of private, voluntary and parochial institutions be harnessed in furthering public safety?

Meeting the regulatory challenges

The introduction of the SIA affords the promise of a higher-quality and more closely regulated private security industry, as respondents to our survey of security firms testify. The SIA has a key role in developing the professionalism to improve standards, training and competencies, and public legitimacy of the private security industry. In regulating the industry, it should seek to articulate how the development of effective partnerships with local police will be of some benefit and importance to the industry's future.

Nevertheless, in much of the private security field, there appears to be little differentiation in terms of quality, with cost being a defining feature. This requires a shift in attitudes on behalf of both potential purchasers and providers towards a focus on the quality and efficacy of policing, regardless of who provides it. The work done by the British Security Industry Association's Police and Public Services Section, for example, demonstrates that there are those within the industry willing to embrace a more active engagement with public policing. The capacity of the SIA to deliver robust regulation will be essential in promoting a security industry that can be trusted by the police, other security providers and the public. Local police need to work with both the SIA and the regulated private security industry to improve levels of trust.

The government's ideas for reinvigorating community engagement and strengthening local accountability arrangements, as set out in the consultation document *Policing: Building safer communities together*, largely remain located within a narrow conception of policing as something that, by and large, the police alone do. The government's proposals for local Community Safety Boards and (force-level) Strategic Policing Boards are police-centred and statutory authority-dominated. Interestingly, however, nearly three quarters (73%) of all respondents to the government's consultation questionnaire indicated that they favoured accountability arrangements that cover wider community safety issues than merely oversight of the police service alone (Home Office, 2004b, p 29).

The development of local and regional policing boards capable of providing oversight and coordination of plural policing arrangements would be in keeping with the government's proposals to consider "whether to broaden the current oversight arrangements beyond just the police service itself and look at **community safety in a wider sense** – to ensure that the performance of other partners and agencies, not just the police, are responsible for community safety" (Home Office, 2003, p 23; emphasis in original). Unfortunately, the government has preferred to ignore or sideline these wider issues in its latest plans for policing reform as set out in the *Building communities, beating crime* White Paper, which remains stubbornly narrow in its police-centred view of policing (Home Office, 2004d).

Local accountability

Accountability to local beneficiaries will demand the provision of good-quality information about policing and patrol activities and feedback on local initiatives. This may be implied within or expressly required by local security contracts or agreements with private, municipal or public providers. The broad nature of the roles fulfilled by many patrol personnel renders simple performance measurement rather crude and sometimes unhelpful. Performance indicators often focus on administrative rather than operational issues – such as numbers of visits made, hours spent on the street, etc – and measure outputs rather than outcomes. In part, this may be due to the fact that community safety outcomes are not easily measurable, nor is it appropriate to attribute simple cause-and-effect relationships in a field in which diverse agencies can have an influence and where complex social and economic processes are involved.

It should not be forgotten that the performance measurement culture within the police service over the past decade has done much to undermine reassurance policing and the dedication of police officers to visible local patrols, by pulling them into more easily measurable, reactive tasks. Nevertheless, creative use of performance measurement that focuses on the stated purposes and key activities of the role can provide motivation and encourage officers to value certain aspects of their work, such as encouraging crime prevention, problem solving and community engagement.

Crime and disorder reduction partnerships

There are now 354 crime and disorder reduction partnerships (CDRPs) in England and 22 community safety partnerships in Wales. The effectiveness of partnerships is variable across the country. Despite the rhetoric, local community safety partnerships have largely failed to engage in any significant way with the private sector (HMIC, 2000). They almost exclusively incorporate public sector agencies and to a lesser degree the voluntary sector. Some partnerships struggle to secure an active contribution from key public sector agencies. However, CDRPs remain a vital mechanism for delivering and coordinating community safety. As such, they can afford important accountability and oversight of plural policing and assume a role analogous to a local policing board.

The government is correct to acknowledge that more needs to be done to strengthen the visibility, role, accountability and local responsiveness of CDRPs. To this end, it has announced a review of the partnership provisions of the 1998 Crime and Disorder Act and proposes to publish a wider Community Safety Strategy in 2005. It is hoped that this review will grasp the opportunity to consider holistic arrangements for local oversight and coordination of plural policing.

Regional policing boards

It is at the regional level that a policing board might have the most impact. This would allow for oversight of the community safety activities of diverse policing providers. It would foster the coordination of efforts across, as well as within, force boundaries. The recent concentration of political resources at the level of regional government offices, notably through regional crime and disorder reduction directorates, suggests that this would be an appropriate place to locate such activities. Regional policing boards might support the SIA in its licensing endeavours, acting as local administrative sites for operational enforcement. Simultaneously, they could act to oversee and standardise accreditation schemes, removing the burden from the police themselves. This would serve to bring into closer alignment the two forms of regulation and thereby help to reduce any emerging inconsistencies.

A regional policing board could ensure greater standardisation of quality among plural providers by working with other relevant authorities over the nature and extent of service provision, thus reducing the potential for conflicts of interest to arise from the dualism of the police's current market role as 'regulator-cum-provider'. A regional policing board would remove from individual Chief Constables the responsibility for, and burden of, accreditation. It would also address the concerns of Chief Constables over their potential vicarious liability with regard to accredited community safety officers as well as provide strategic oversight and coordination of the public, municipal, commercial and voluntary agencies that comprise local policing networks.

The potential advent of regional assemblies might allow regional policing boards to connect with lines of democratic accountability. A regional policing board as one tier of oversight, coordination and regulation would also pre-empt any subsequent shifts towards regional police forces and map onto the regional bases of private sector developments.

Potential implications of reassurance policing through public–private partnerships

The research highlights a number of implications arising from close public–private partnerships.

Increase demands on the public police: The 'eyes and ears' function of visible patrol officers can serve to increase demand on the police organisation as a whole. It may do so by generating greater information on the basis of increased surveillance that requires a response. It may also identify new needs arising from a lower threshold of tolerance and the policing of previously neglected anti-social behaviour. Furthermore, servicing public–private partnerships and parochial clubbing endeavours can place additional burdens on the public police.

Draw public policing resources away from crime-related need into responding to subjective fears: Police as a public resource may be drawn into policing low-level incivilities in areas where fear of crime is high but the incidence of crime is low and, hence, away from areas with more serious crime problems. The current emphasis on reassurance policing has the capacity to skew resources away from crime need and into areas where there are high levels of anxiety and perceived risk.

Present a dichotomy of response from police forces: The public may come to perceive an ambiguous response from the police whereby, on the one hand, the police focus on low-level disorder (through CSO deployment in particular) while, on the other hand, the public may receive little or no response to more serious high-volume crime, as many police forces are routinely required to screen out what members of the public regard as relatively serious crimes.

Represent a bifurcation of policing, relegating the sworn police constable to a residual confrontational role: The proactive, preventative, community-facing and non-confrontational side of policing may be hived off to visible patrol personnel, be they CSOs, wardens or private security, while the reactive, fire-brigade style and confrontational aspects of policing remain with sworn police constables. This bifurcation of the 'soft' and 'hard' faces of policing may affect the relationship between police and public. This scenario might see sworn officers having less contact with the public relying more on policing by coercion, leaving policing by consent to other patrolling staff. The gradual retreat of police officers from non-conflictual interaction with the public may have adverse implications for public trust if they come to be seen as little more than an 'arrest service'.

Encourage an assumption that responsive, locally tied visible patrols are additional to 'normal' policing and, as such, require separate funding: There is a growing acknowledgement, albeit in some instances a resentful one, on the part of businesses, local authorities, housing associations and residents' groups that if they want a visible patrol presence in their locality or neighbourhood capable of responding to their needs, they will have to pay for it. This raises significant questions about access to the market for additional patrol services and the appropriate distribution of policing and patrols. If access is primarily determined by the capacity to pay, we may well see some areas enjoy a surfeit of security while others experience a policing deficit.

Foster different expectations of service: This may occur indirectly through the fostering of a more instrumental and commercial judgement of policing. Policing may be perceived to 'work' if it delivers visible and tangible results that are meaningful to citizens. This may depend on the capacity of providers to deliver a measurable service to a determined level of quality that consumers can appreciate and value.

Dilute the symbolic authority of the police: Public acknowledgement of a mixed economy of plural policing may puncture the image of the omnicompetent British 'bobby' and deflate the revered (yet idealised) status of the constable. For the public, a tangible expression of this concern is to be found in the dilution of the 'police brand' reflected in diverse uniforms that are similar to or ape police uniforms to a greater or lesser degree. Our research revealed considerable public uncertainties over uniforms and identities. Furthermore, as patrol personnel, other than sworn constables, increasingly become the visible public face of policing, any misconduct or lapses in standards of ethics on their part may adversely impact on the police as a whole. This may be particularly evident where such officers are employed or accredited by the police themselves. As such, the police may lose further control of their own fate. Moreover, given the absence of clarity over officers' responsibilities, powers and limitations, the public often assumes that visible patrol personnel can act like police officers, an assumption that may be found wanting in practice.

Raise the (in)security threshold: The provision of additional policing may serve to highlight the perception of a crime-related problem and heighten levels of anxiety, particularly in places with relatively low levels of crime. The short-term emphasis on providing high levels of visibility may ignore the fact that long-term reassurance is more complex, concerned with the quality of public interactions as well as the skills and competencies of officers to negotiate situations. Reassurance, like trust, may take considerable time and effort to construct and maintain but may be brittle and easily fractured.

Raise false expectations over security: Patrol-based responses to insecurity problems and dilemmas of disorder may encourage a false belief in policing solutions alone, ignoring or failing to tackle more fundamental and structural social or economic issues that lie behind and inform these problems. Ultimately, policing efforts are but an element in the wider framework of fostering vibrant and orderly communities. Merely responding to demands for greater security through the provision of additional policing and patrol personnel may fail to engage with and negotiate the nature of these demands.

The future of visible policing

Future relations between the police and other plural policing providers and personnel are likely to be structured around a number of ideal typical forms (see Crawford, 2003, p 157):

* an integrationist model;
* a steering model;
* a networked model; and
* a market model.

An integrationist model is one in which forms of policing are integrated within the police organisation and in which the vast majority of patrolling services are provided through the public police. Here, the police directly employ a larger proportion of the security workforce, notably patrol personnel. CSOs are a prime example of this expansion of the police fold.

A steering model exists where the police seek to 'govern at a distance' the policing activities of plural providers. Here, the police sit at the apex of a pyramid structure but do not directly employ patrol personnel. In this model, the police are both ideologically and legally dominant. This model assumes a relationship in which policing beyond the police serves as the professional police's 'junior partner' (Cunningham and Taylor, 1985). A key element in this strategy is the accreditation by the police of the policing activities of others. Accredited community safety officers will only partly be under police direction. Accreditation represents a form of 'arm's-length' governance, with advantages for the police. It potentially allows a response to public demand for high-visibility reassurance policing, without the cost. Accreditation also facilitates the responsibilisation of private organisations by encouraging them to take greater account of, and responsibility for, their own policing and security matters.

A networked model is one in which plural policing providers link together in horizontal partnerships in the co-production of local security. Divergent forms of policing are loosely connected through networks and alliances. No particular provider within the network is accorded a dominant role. Nevertheless, this model presupposes an element of coordination. In theory, if not in practice, CDRPs as local community safety partnerships have advanced the local infrastructure for such a networked model.

A market model exists where competition structures the relations between divergent providers. This model suggests the need for an independent regulatory agency above and outside of the competing parties to ensure fair competition and appropriate standards, and to safeguard the public interest, notably where the market fails to provide adequately or appropriately.

Our research found examples of all these models, sometimes coexisting in more or less awkward relations. In large part, this ambiguity is reflected in central as well as local government policies and programmes. Each model is to be found to some degree in the current patchwork of plural policing and recent policy initiatives. However, contrary to the claims of some recent international academic literature (Johnston and Shearing, 2003), our research found little evidence of a networked model of policing as a dominant or prevailing reality. Furthermore, we can identify two additional trends:

Relations are likely to become more, rather than less, competitive, notably given government's commitment to expand the number of CSOs to 24,000 by 2008. Uncertainties over the future funding of CSOs will necessitate police forces to look to external income generation to support this expansion. Competition within the private security sector in the light of the introduction of regulation is likely to concentrate market activity and may see some shift from manned security to technological solutions, through gating, access control and surveillance systems.

The expanding number of CSOs presents police forces with a considerable cultural challenge to integrate CSOs into the wider service. To this end, it is uncertain to what extent the CSO role will be able to maintain a distinct yet integrated identity within the police. In the rush to recruit and meet government targets, sight may be lost of the important qualities, skills and competencies required of the role. Experiences from the across the country (notably the Metropolitan Police) caution against too rapid or dramatic an expansion in CSO numbers, given the need to ensure high-quality recruits. As CSOs increasingly become the public face of the police, high standards of CSO conduct and disposition in interactions with the public are vital in order to establish and maintain confidence in their work and thus ensure long-term public reassurance. Thorough consideration needs to be given to the manner in which CSOs engage with the diverse communities they police rather than merely patrolling like 'mobile scarecrows'. Furthermore, if CSO-generated community intelligence is to be used effectively by the police organisation, this will require its careful integration into systems of information management and data analysis.

CSO recruitment places significant management challenges on the police. The support infrastructures within the police need to be prepared for the additional burdens that increased numbers of CSOs will bring, including supervision and intelligence analysis. Flooding streets with poorly prepared and weakly supported recruits may prove counterproductive. The central challenge for the future management of CSOs will be to resist pressures to use them as a generic resource to fill service gaps within the organisation rather than as a strategic tool in the provision of public reassurance, crime prevention and community engagement. Given the government's substantial expansion plans and proposals to expand significantly CSOs' powers, this may prove difficult.

Conclusions and recommendations

7

A number of governments around the world have recognised the need to think afresh about the provision and regulation of contemporary policing, notably with regard to the visible patrol function and relations between the diverse public, municipal and private providers. Recent government-sponsored reviews in the US, Canada and, to a lesser degree, Northern Ireland (Patten, 1999; Bayley and Shearing, 2001; Law Commission of Canada, 2002) have sought to encompass a broader understanding of policing, incorporating the activities of those beyond the police. Traditionally, in England and Wales, this debate has tended to be restricted to the activities and regulation of the police and hence to 'police reform'. Now is an appropriate time for a considered review of the nature, contribution and social implications of visible policing both within and beyond the police, one that takes stock of recent ad hoc developments and incorporates a concern for public safety in its widest sense.

For too long, governments have thought of solutions to public anxieties in narrow terms of police and criminal justice reform and police officer numbers. It is no longer realistic to think of policing in terms of public police forces alone. There is now an urgent need to open up this debate to embrace a holistic understanding of policing. The contemporary challenge is to harness the diverse efforts of plural policing providers and auspices in the furtherance of public safety, without allowing the vagaries of unequal access and differentiated provision – fuelled by security as a commodity – in a weakly regulated market to segregate populations further along lines demarcated by their capacity to purchase additional security or retreat from the public sphere.

Recommendations

- Government should consider ways to clarify the division of labour and address the blurring of roles across different forms of plural policing. It should review the current workings of the segmented mechanisms for regulating plural policing, with a view to joining up the various forms of governance. More fundamentally, it needs to reflect on whether new policy initiatives encourage conditions that foster and sustain joint partnerships and collaborative local action.

- Consideration should be given to establishing regional policing boards with responsibility for coordinating service delivery across plural policing providers and regulating the distribution and impact of security markets. Regional policing boards could also provide a degree of democratic accountability where regional assemblies exist.

- Local crime and disorder reduction partnerships should be encouraged to engage more fully with the private sector and assist in the task of coordinating local policing services, providing local oversight of plural policing arrangements and strengthening local accountability.

- Private security firms need to engage constructively with the new regulatory regime and the Security Industry Authority's implementation. If the security sector is to become a significant partner in community safety, it needs to grasp the opportunity presented by regulation to drive up standards, improve practice and secure greater public confidence.

- Consideration should be given to greater public awareness and standardisation of uniforms for community support officers (CSOs) and clearer badging for accredited private security officers and wardens, to address problems of public confusion and uncertainty over what can legitimately be expected of specific personnel.

- The work of CSOs, their place within the police and contribution to community safety need clarification and evaluation before significant or rapid expansion. Otherwise, CSOs are likely to suffer 'mission creep' and be drawn into diverse roles that may undermine their reassurance value.

- The policy of giving patrol personnel increased powers, specifically fixed penalty notices, needs to be reviewed in the light of possible adverse impacts this may have on public interactions and the central tasks of each type of officer.

- Police forces should consider institutional ways in which they can better engage with the 'extended police family' and integrate civilian staff.

- Police forces need to develop more systematic and structured approaches to the collection, storage and use of community intelligence.

- Clearer career paths within and between police officers and civilian staff, warden schemes and private security should be mapped out, allowing for different points of entry and transfer of skills.

- In the light of recent case law, government should consider reviewing whether property law rights of landowners to exclude people without any test for reasonableness are appropriate in the context of modern 'quasi-public' spaces such as shopping malls and leisure centres.

References

ACPO (Association of Chief Police Officers) (2004) *A guide to income generation for the police service in England & Wales*, London: ACPO.

Audit Commission (1992) *Fine lines: Improving the traffic warden service*, London: Audit Commission.

Bayley, D. and Shearing, C. (2001) *The new structure of policing*, Washington DC: National Institute of Justice.

Bichard, M. (2004) *The Bichard Inquiry Report*, London: The Stationery Office.

Bittner, E. (1967) 'The police on skid row: a study in peacekeeping', *American Sociological Review*, vol 32, pp 600-715.

BSIA (British Security Industry Association) (2001) 'Interesting facts and figures in the UK security industry', www.bsia.co.uk/industry.html

Button, M. (2002) *Private policing*, Cullompton: Willan.

Christophersen, O. and Cotton, J. (2004) *Police service strength, England and Wales*, London: Home Office.

Cope, N. (2004) 'Intelligence led policing or policing led intelligence?', *British Journal of Criminology*, vol 44, no 2, pp 188-203.

Crawford, A. (1998) *Crime prevention and community safety*, Harlow: Longman.

Crawford, A. (2003) 'The pattern of policing in the UK: policing beyond the police', in T. Newburn (ed) *Handbook of policing*, Cullompton: Willan, pp 136-68.

Crawford, A. and Lister, S. (2004) *The extended policing family*, York: Joseph Rowntree Foundation.

Crawford, A., Lister, S. and Wall, D. (2003) *Great expectations: Contracted community policing in New Earswick*, York: Joseph Rowntree Foundation.

Crawford, A., Blackburn, S., Lister, S. and Shepherd, P. (2004) *Patrolling with a purpose: An evaluation of police community support officers in Leeds and Bradford city centres*, Leeds: CCJS Press.

Cunningham, W.C. and Taylor, T. (1985) *Private security and police in America*, Boston, MA: Heinemann.

Dodd, T., Nicholas, S., Povey, D. and Walker, A. (2004) *Crime in England and Wales 2003/2004*, London: Home Office.

Ericson, R. and Haggerty, K. (1997) *Policing the risk society*, Oxford: Clarendon.

Fitzgerald, M., Hough, M., Joseph, I. and Qureshi, T. (2002) *Policing for London*, Cullompton: Willan.

HMIC (Her Majesty's Inspectorate of Constabulary) (2000) *Calling time on crime: A thematic inspection on crime and disorder*, London: HMIC.

HMIC (2004) *Modernising the Police Service*, London: HMIC.

Home Office (2003) *Policing: Building safer communities together*, London: Home Office.

Home Office (2004a) *Confident communities in a secure Britain: The Home Office Strategic Plan 2004-08*, Cm 6287, London: Home Office.

Home Office (2004b) *Policing: Building safer communities together: Summary of consultation response*, London: Home Office.

Home Office (2004c) *Policing: Modernising police powers to meet community needs*, London: Home Office.

Home Office (2004d) *Building communities, beating crime*, London: Home Office.

Innes, M. (2004) 'Reassurance and neighbourhood policing', Paper presented at the Plural Policing Conference, Church House, London, 28 October.

Johnston, L. (1993) *The rebirth of private policing*, London: Routledge.

Johnston, L. and Shearing, C. (2003) *Governing security*, London: Routledge.

Jones, T. and Newburn, T. (1998) *Private security and public policing*, Oxford: Clarendon Press.

Jones, T. and Newburn, T. (2002) 'The transformation of policing? Understanding current trends in policing systems', *British Journal of Criminology*, vol 42, no 1, pp 129-46.

Law Commission of Canada (2002) *In search of security: The roles of public police and private agencies*, Ottowa: Law Commission.

Lister, S., Wall, D. and Bryan, J. (2004) *Evaluation of the Leeds Distraction Burglary Initiative*, Home Office Online Report 44/04, London: Home Office.

Loader, I. (2000) 'Plural policing and democratic governance', *Social & Legal Studies*, vol 9, no 3, pp 323-45.

Minton, A. (2002) *Building balanced communities: The US and UK compared*, London: Royal Institution of Chartered Surveyors.

Mirrlees-Black, C. (2001) *Confidence in the criminal justice system: Findings from the 2000 British Crime Survey*, London: Home Office.

ODPM (Office of the Deputy Prime Minister) (2002) *Living places: Cleaner, safer, greener*, London: ODPM.

ODPM (2004) *Neighbourhood Wardens Scheme Evaluation, Research Report 8*, London: ODPM.

PA Consulting Group (2001) *Diary of a police officer*, London: Home Office.

Page, B., Wake, R. and Ames, A. (2004) *Public confidence in the criminal justice system, Findings 221*, London: Home Office.

Patten, C. (1999) *A new beginning: Policing in Northern Ireland, Report of the Independent Commission on Policing for Northern Ireland*, London: The Stationery Office.

Povey, K. (2001) *Open all hours*, London: HMIC.

Putnam, R. (2000) *Bowling alone*, New York, NY: Touchstone.

Rhodes, R.A.W. (1996) 'The new governance: governing without government', *Political Studies*, vol 44, pp 652-67.

Sampson, R.J., Raudenbush, S.W. and Earls, F. (1997) 'Neighborhoods and violent crime: a multi-level study of collective efficacy', *Science*, vol 277, pp 918-23.

SEU (Social Exclusion Unit) (1998) *Bringing Britain together: A national strategy for neighbourhood renewal*, London: Cabinet Office.

SEU (2001) *National strategy for neighbourhood renewal*, London: Cabinet Office.

Shearing, C. (2000) '"A new beginning" for policing', *Journal of Law and Society*, vol 27, no 3, pp 386-93.

Shearing, C. and Stenning, P. (1981) 'Modern private security: its growth and implications', *Crime & Justice*, vol 3, pp 193-245.

Simmons, J. and Dodd, T. (eds) (2003) *Crime in England and Wales 2002/3, Statistical Bulletin 07/03*, London: Home Office.

Singer, L. (2004) *Community support officer (detention power) pilot: evaluation results*, London: Home Office.

Tyler, T. (1998) 'Trust and democratic governance', in V. Braithwaite and M. Levi (eds) *Trust and governance*, New York, NY: Russell Sage Foundation, pp 269-94.

Von Hirsch, A. and Shearing, C. (2000) 'Exclusion from public space', in A. Von Hirsch, D. Garland and A. Wakefield (eds) *Ethical and social perspectives on situational crime prevention*, Oxford: Hart Publishing, pp 77-96.

Wakefield, A. (2003) *Selling security: The private policing of public space*, Cullompton: Willan.

Appendix A:
The case study sites

Bradford City Centre

The Metropolitan District of Bradford has a population of almost 500,000, although approximately five million people live within a 30-mile radius of the city centre. Nine of the district's 30 council wards fall within the most deprived 10% of England and Wales. The city has a high ethnic mix, with almost 20% of its population of Asian origin, although this rises to approximately 50% within the inner-city areas. The city centre has a daily transient population of 150,000 workers, shoppers and tourists. It has few residential developments, but more than 500 retail outlets.

The diverse forms of visible patrol personnel in the city centre included: 418 West Yorkshire Police (WYP) officers (including 343 constables and 51 sergeants) and 170 police staff operating from the division; 54 special constables available for voluntary duties; 30 community support officers (CSOs) deployed in March 2003 (by March 2004, this number had risen to 34); 12 street wardens; 15 WYP traffic wardens; eight council-employed parking attendants; and a significant number of private security guards, notably in the shopping centres and markets.

Two Basic Command Units police the city. The first cohort of 30 CSOs was deployed from March 2003 to Bradford South Division, which includes the city centre, the university and the main sports stadia. The initial wave of CSOs patrolled eight city centre beats within the Bradford South Division. After three weeks of initial training in Wakefield, CSOs were placed with a mentor, a regular constable, who could offer advice and support for the first two weeks. CSOs were grouped into four teams of seven or eight and placed with regular police teams within the division. CSOs worked nine-hour shifts between 8am and 3am. They patrolled individually until 5.00pm or when it gets dark (in winter months) beyond which they patrolled in pairs. CSOs were supervised by two sergeants and one inspector. CSOs were given traffic wardens' powers and detention powers. They were issued with a stab vest, notebook and police radio.

The street wardens were funded through the Office of the Deputy Prime Minister and the Neighbourhood Renewal Fund. They covered a similar deployment area as CSOs and were also based at Bradford Central police station (The Tyrlls) in same office. Street wardens work early or late shifts between 8.30am and 7.30pm each day of the week and usually patrol individually. They are connected to the City Centre Link and CCTV systems but have no police radio access. They have mobile phones and stab vests. Unlike their colleagues in Leeds, they have not yet applied for accreditation status from WYP.

WYP established a Plural Policing Unit, officially launched in March 2004, with the purpose of encouraging the convergence of the wider 'policing family' and disseminating good practice across the force with regard to civilian and volunteer members of WYP. The unit includes a number of key staff including a head (a chief inspector); a project manager; a CSO liaison trainer; a coordinator; and an Anti-Social Behaviour Unit coordinator. The unit assumed responsibility for CSO recruitment, training, allocation, funding and liaison with divisions, as well as the accreditation of other plural policing providers.

Overall crime declined by 10% in the first year of CSO deployment (April 2003 to March 2004), as against the previous year. The total number of vehicle-related crime declined by 19% – theft from a vehicle fell by 23%, theft of vehicle by 25% and vehicle interference and tampering by 24% – while personal robbery declined by 46%, albeit from a low base. Whereas theft declined by 20%, violent crime increased by 16%, reflecting wider national trends. For most types of crime, there does not appear to have been a significant displacement effect, albeit that some geographical displacement was apparent with regard to theft from a vehicle.

Liverpool Gold Zones

After a significant bidding process, Liverpool was successfully awarded the status of European Capital of Culture, 2008. It has a burgeoning city centre, which attracts roughly seven million visitors a year, and has a working population of more than 75,000. The centre is home to approximately 500 retail stores and 180 licensed premises and is increasingly popular as a residential setting.

In 1998 the city centre was divided into 'Gold Zones', an initiative that has been replicated since in other cities. The Gold Zone scheme originally emerged in conjunction with a commitment to the urban regeneration and renewal of the city centre. Partner agencies include Liverpool Vision and Cityfocus. There are now six Gold Zones, with the stated aims of 'cleaning up, brightening up, and speaking up'. In 2000, the Gold Zone initiative was supplemented by the Gold Zone policing initiative, through which 12 local authority-funded police officers are dedicated to particular Gold Zones.

A sergeant, match-funded by Merseyside Police, oversaw the 12 officers. They were expected to patrol their designated Gold Zones and foster contacts with businesses, while simultaneously maintaining a high-visibility policing presence. This was in addition to the presence of 'normal' Merseyside Police officers in the city centre. From the end of 2003, street wardens also patrolled the city centre and had beats that loosely corresponded with the Gold Zones. The street wardens replaced local authority-funded 'navigators' who previously combined a 'meeting and greeting' the public role with enforcing particular by-laws that are prominent within the city centre, notably skate boarding and fly posting in areas where such activities are banned. Many of the retail stores in the city centre employ private security officers, and similarly, in the evening, door supervisors and bouncers are employed in many of the pubs and clubs.

A number of initiatives were established around the framework of Gold Zones policing. In particular, Operation Change and Operation Crystal Clear had very high profiles and received considerable media attention. Operation Change was a multi-agency initiative that combined the provision of support to homeless people in the city centre with a 'zero-tolerance' approach to any criminal activity. Operation Crystal Clear responded to the high level of injuries sustained at night in the city centre involving smashed drinking glasses. Again, this was a multi-agency initiative and has been replicated in many city centres in the UK. Other, less well-known, policing initiatives included Operation Ringlet aimed at Big Issue sellers fraudulently claiming benefits; Fresher, involving the safety of new students to the city; and Coinage, concerning theft from parking meters.

Information exchange between policing providers in the Gold Zones is facilitated primarily through Crime Alert meetings, an initiative overseen by Business Crime Direct affiliated to the Chamber of Commerce. Membership provides a number of benefits that include privileged access to information on offenders in the area and a radio link that connects businesses with particular policing agencies in the vicinity. Meetings provide opportunities to share information about offenders, and the initiative has a night-time counterpart, Nite-Alert.

The city centre is set to become a Business Improvement District, in which businesses will pay a levy for services including the provision of security. It is estimated that this may impact on the priorities of Gold Zone policing, and further increase the number of policing bodies within the centre.

MetroCentre, Gateshead

MetroCentre, Gateshead is one of Europe's largest out-of-town shopping and leisure centres, attracting 25 million visitors a year, and employing more than 6,000 people. The centre attracts 40,000 vehicles per day and has 300 shops, a theme park, bowling alley, cinemas, restaurants and pubs.

Historically, the MetroCentre was perceived as problematic for Northumbria Police, not least due to high incidences of car crime. In 2002, the centre was one of the first major shopping centres in Britain to enter into an agreement with its local police authority to finance a team of community beat managers (CBMs) at a cost of £130,000 per year. Eight uniformed police officers were selected and trained to adopt the role of 'village bobby' within the centre, and are overseen directly by a police sergeant. Each officer has his or her own beat, with the aim of establishing a regular rapport with the retailers and shoppers to manage crime and disorder. There is a small police station located within the MetroCentre.

This policing initiative originated as a partnership involving Northumbria Police, the MetroCentre, and St James' Security, a contracted security firm. St James' Security complements the police presence with a total of 64 officers. These officers are further split into subgroups covering the 'malls', the service yards and the car parks. Furthermore, each subgroup has slightly different priorities aimed at the particular needs of a given part of the centre. For example, those officers on the 'malls' are encouraged to provide a highly visible presence for members of the public, while certain officers in the car parks are wholly dedicated to crime within this vicinity.

Additional policing is provided through the centre's own security, the X-ray team. This team of covert officers focuses predominantly, but not exclusively, on theft from stores within the centre. A small number of stores also employ their own in-house security officers. Certain leisure outlets, such as the MetroLand, also incorporate security functions within the roles of their staff generally.

A number of strategies have been generated through the MetroCentre policing initiative. The initiative is integrated within a Safer Shopping Partnership, which aims to encourage stores to contribute to their own crime prevention, primarily through regular information-sharing meetings. Further initiatives include working with local schools to provide a discount 'SMART card' scheme for well-behaved pupils, liaison with the Youth Offending Service to undertake supervised community service around the site, and the formation of partnerships with retail crime prevention organisations in Newcastle, Gateshead, Durham and Cleveland. The centre has pioneered the innovative use of a radio-link system to target police resources.

The initiative was initially due to run until 2005, but is likely to continue beyond this time given its perceived success. Also, the number of bodies performing policing functions is expected to increase as the centre itself expands. For example, traffic wardens may be employed in 2005 to bolster the crime prevention strategies within the car parks.

Since the scheme was launched in 2002, car crime has been reduced by 17% and shop theft has decreased by 52%. In 2003, the MetroCentre's management team was recognised as the Northumbria Police Community 'Partner of the Year' for its pioneering security initiatives.

Trafford Park Industrial Estate, Greater Manchester

Trafford Park is Europe's largest industrial estate, covering approximately 1,183 acres. The estate suffered considerable decline following the Second World War, and this continued until 1987 when the Trafford Park Development Corporation (TPDC) began a substantial regeneration project within its vicinity. The TPDC formally disbanded in 1998, but had by that point attracted more than 1,000 new companies and £1.759 billion of private sector investment. Some 1,600 businesses now operate within Trafford Park and between them they employ approximately 53,000 people.

Despite the considerable regeneration of the area, Trafford Park continued to suffer disproportionately high rates of criminal victimisation, notably in the form of commercial burglaries. This prompted the Home Office to provide £456,000 in 2001 to fund the two-year Trafford Park Security Initiative (TPSI). The TPSI was set up in part to reduce this rate of criminal incidences, and also to establish the estate as an environment where businesses could flourish.

The TPSI was a partnership consisting of Greater Manchester Police, Trafford Borough Council, Trafford Park Business Watch, and latterly Noble Security, a private security company. The initiative funded a project manager, a dedicated crime analyst, two 'business wardens' and a number of police operations within the vicinity of the estate. These operations were further supplemented by the presence of two dedicated police officers.

A number of further initiatives were instigated under the auspices of the TPSI, which related to the specific policing priorities of Trafford Park itself. The most publicised of these was the Guardsafe scheme, a voluntary registration and training scheme for security officers. This scheme was heralded as a precursor to the new licensing regime being introduced under the 2001 Private Security Industry Act. Approximately 100 security companies operate within the estate, and employ roughly 2,500 security officers. Overseen by the combined presence of Noble Security, the local authority and Greater Manchester police, Guardsafe aimed to harness and coordinate this policing presence.

Alongside the Guardsafe scheme ran a Business Watch initiative. Although this had been active since the 1980s, the TPSI funded a full-time manager to improve its efficiency and impact. Business Watch acted as a conduit between police, businesses, and the local authority. It aimed to improve the flow of information around crime and crime prevention activities between these bodies, and also to encourage businesses to join Business Watch and receive the benefits that were said to derive from this.

Other initiatives included Patrol Net, where a security company provided a patrol service within the estate and the promise of a rapid response to criminal activity. Furthermore, the TPSI encouraged a number of 'responsibilisation' strategies, such as the part funding of Best Practice Estates, where businesses were encouraged to club together and create defensible spaces. Some of the strategies harnessed within the TPSI pre-dated the initiative itself, and others have outlived it in other forms. The TPSI has now finished, and its impacts may be assessed by the increasing level of recorded criminal activity since its demise.

Halton Moor Estate, Leeds

The Halton Moor estate is located in the Richmond Hill ward of East Leeds and comprises more than 2,500 residents in over 1,100 properties, more than three quarters of which are council- or housing association-owned. There are few shops or business premises on the estate, which has a greater proportion of minors (32%) than is the norm for Leeds. There are fewer adults of working age and nearly a third of the population is aged over 45 years. There are over twice as many lone parent families than in Leeds as a whole, partly explaining the atypical age structure. The area is predominantly white (97% according to 2001 Census data), has an unemployment rate of just under 10% and 63% of people aged 16-74 have no educational qualifications. Part of the area comprises a designated Single Regeneration Budget (SRB) area. In material deprivation terms, 70% of people within the estate as a whole are living within the top 10% most deprived areas in Leeds (2001 Census). For social deprivation, 59% of people are living within the top 10% most deprived areas in Leeds. Twice as many households are in receipt of council-administered benefits than is the norm for Leeds.

Historically, the estate has experienced significant problems with crime, fear of crime, anti-social behaviour, truancy and void properties. Levels of recorded vehicle-related crime and burglary are double the national average. Arson is a particular problem, although rates for arson against vehicles and properties have fallen in recent years. Deliberate primary fires occur at four times the rate across Leeds and 2.5 times for secondary fires. Abandoned vehicles are another by-product of the vehicle arson problem. The rate of cars collected by Leeds City Council is more than twice the Leeds norm. The recent council crime audit found that, over the past two years, crime levels have declined by 11%. The audit also revealed that fear of crime in the area had increased, over the same period, by 50%.

Neighbourhood wardens, public police and private security all work within the estate. Historically, residents have complained about the lack of police presence on the estate. A security firm (Mayfair Guarding) provides night-time, mobile patrols, sometimes recording incidents via an on-board video camera. This evidence is made available to the police and other relevant agencies, if requested. Mayfair Guarding is the third private security firm to provide patrols since early 2002. Previously, the council's in-house security service patrolled the estate with an emphasis on monitoring void properties and graffiti.

In February 2002, two centrally funded neighbourhood wardens were deployed on Halton Moor. In December 2002, this was reduced when one of the team (considered particularly experienced at working on difficult estates) was moved to another 'problematic' estate in Leeds, and subsequently not replaced. The remaining warden, who works exclusively during the daytime, liaises closely with residents' groups and other local service providers, exchanging information over environmental, housing and community matters. The estate has a community beat officer to develop problem-solving approaches to crime.

In summer 2004, a second warden was moved onto the estate as a result of city-wide staff reorganisation, in part because original funding from the Office of the Deputy Prime Minister was coming to an end and a number of areas with wardens opted to use council funding to employ community support officers (CSOs). The local community involvement team (CIT) consulted with other teams that chose CSOs, but elected not to follow their lead. Rather, wardens were promised assistance in finding alternative employment where jobs were to be cut (eight warden posts were lost across Leeds). A number were relocated to other council posts and one transferred to become a street warden. Under a recent council reorganisation, prompted by the new political make-up of the council in the light of the June 2004 elections, CITs are being replaced by area committees, with the intention of decentralising decision making and resource allocation, including placing community safety under a 'well-being' budget linked to council priorities but with flexibility for local discretion.

The Youth Offending Service (YOS) and Anti-Social Behaviour Unit (ASBU) have a presence in the area and liaise with the neighbourhood warden through service meetings, albeit not very closely. There are twice the number of young people on the books of the YOS than the Leeds average. For the ASBU, the lack of relevant information from residents is a source of frustration, stymieing joint operations by police and housing services and the ASBU. The estate has benefited from city-wide initiatives, including the Smart Water project funded by Leeds community safety, a property-marking scheme, and LEAP, an environmental clean-up operation. Ten CCTV cameras were installed on the estate in March 2004. The £260,000 scheme was put into place using Estate Action funding following public and agency consultation. The cameras have been used to gather evidence in the preparation of Anti-social Behaviour Orders.

Foxwood, York

Located to the south-west of York, the Foxwood estate comprises 1,500 low-rise households. The estate grew from a nucleus of local authority properties 20 years ago, with more recent private and housing association development. There are now four social housing providers on the estate. Foxwood is embedded in the wider Wesfield local authority ward, which is ranked 1,714th out of the 9,310 council wards in England and Wales in the indices of deprivation of 2000. Traditionally, the estate has had a relatively poor reputation and above-average crime rates. Over the past five years, however, there has been considerable resident participation in developing community structures and overseeing local service provision.

Private security guards called community rangers have patrolled residential areas of York since 2000, having been initially introduced to the Clifton area of the city, as funded by SRB. Publicity generated from this scheme triggered significant interest among residents and politicians in other parts of the city, and within two years of the initial scheme commencing, 19 of the city's 22 council wards had followed suit. One security company, Mayfair Guarding, is the single supplier to all but one of these wards. Patrol time is purchased from the security company via a devolved council budget, which enables residents to vote annually, thereby determining which local services they wish to fund. As ward committee spending plans are formulated on an annual basis, formal contracts between City of York Council and the security provider(s) are binding for one year only. The council now spends more than £140,000 annually on private security patrols.

The community rangers began patrolling Foxwood in April 2002. A single-manned vehicle patrol, which carries an on-board surveillance camera, patrols 'nuisance youth' hot spots five nights a week. The ward committee purchases two 30-minute patrols, to be provided between 7pm and 9pm and 9pm and midnight, at an annual cost of £3,500 (from an annual devolved Foxwood budget of £17,400). Hot spots are identified by local residents, council officers and community police officers and the rangers themselves. Residents are supplied with the patrol company's contact telephone number, which enables them to summon the rangers to attend to low-level incidents of disorder. The rangers provide monthly activity reports to interested parties that detail incidents they have encountered and attended, as requested either by the police or the public, and incidents they have reported to the police. These are monitored by Safer York Partnership (SYP), which has strategic responsibility for managing and overseeing the city-wide operation of the patrols. The SYP crime reduction officer acts as a conduit, passing information about local disorder hot spots between community police officers and the rangers. In this way, the patrols are steered towards patrolling certain areas of the city.

Council officers suggest that the scheme developed in a non-strategic, ad hoc manner, lacking any formal evaluation. In order to coordinate patrols better and overcome the 'free-rider' problem, council officers wish to issue a purchasing tender for the city-wide patrol service, stipulating only one provider. Council officers have also called on the police to develop protocols in order to clarify the nature and extent of their relationship with the security company. This is due to wide variation in response of police officers within the York Basic Command Unit. In autumn 2003, the Foxwood ward committee voted to continue the purchase of the rangers' service as well as the introduction of CSOs. However, the latter form of patrol has yet to be supplied through a purchasing arrangement because of ongoing negotiations between City of York Council and North Yorkshire Police about operational control over the officers.

Appendix B: The Advisory Board membership

Louise Bennett	Neighbourhood and Street Wardens Unit
Sir Ian Blair	Deputy Commissioner, Metropolitan Police
Richard Childs	Ex-Chief Constable, Lincolnshire Police
David Dickinson	Chairman, British Security Industry Authority
Mike Fagan	Office of the Deputy Prime Minister
Margaret Geary	Regional Crime Reduction Director for the West Midlands
Mark Gore	Chief Superintendent, Metropolitan Police
Peter Hermitage	Chair of Security Industry Authority (from end 2003)
Mike Hough	Professor of Criminology, King's College, London
Anunay Jha	Reassurance Section, Home Office
Mark Liddle	Head of Research, National Association for the Care and Resettlement of Offenders
Molly Meacher	Chair of Security Industry Authority (until end 2003)
Tim Newburn	Professor of Social Policy, London School of Economics
Peter Neyroud	Chief Constable, Thames Valley Police
Les Parrett	Chief Superintendent, Her Majesty's Inspectorate of Constabulary
Robert Reiner	Professor of Criminology, London School of Economics
Lawrence Springall	Police Personnel Unit, Home Office
Jaap de Waard	Director of European Crime Prevention Network
Frank Warburton	Director of Drugscope
Sharon Witherspoon	Deputy Director, The Nuffield Foundation
Carole Willis	Director of Policing & Reducing Crime Unit, Home Office

Youth crime and youth justice
Public opinion in England and Wales

Mike Hough and Julian V. Roberts

This report presents the findings from the first national, representative survey of public attitudes to youth crime and youth justice in England and Wales.

Significantly, it highlights that most people are demonstrably ill-informed about youth crime and youth justice issues. It also carries clear policy implications in relation to both public education and reform of the youth justice system.

Youth crime and youth justice is essential reading for academics, researchers, policy makers and practitioners in the fields of criminal justice, criminology, social policy, social work and probation.

PB £14.99 US$25.00 • ISBN 1 86134 649 2 • 245 x 170mm • 80 pages • November 2004

From dependency to work
Addressing the multiple needs of offenders with drug problems

Tim McSweeney, Victoria Herrington, Mike Hough, Paul J. Turnbull and Jim Parsons

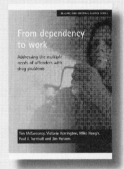

This report presents the findings from one of the first evaluations of a British programme to integrate drug and alcohol treatment with mental health services, and education, training and employment support - the 'From Dependency to Work (D2W)' programme. It provides an invaluable insight into the challenges and difficulties of integrating services in this way and highlights important lessons for central and regional government on funding and working with the voluntary sector to deliver services.

With the recent launch of the Drug Interventions Programme (DIP), designed to get statutory and voluntary sector agencies working together to tackle the social factors associated with drug misuse and crime, stakeholders across the country will need to develop effective multi-disciplinary working in this field. This report provides all those involved, from a strategic level to frontline practitioners, with a clearer understanding of the issues.

PB £14.99 US$25.00 • ISBN 1 86134 660 3 • 245 x 170mm •
88 pages • December 2004

To order further copies of this publication or any other Policy Press titles please contact:

In the UK and Europe:
Marston Book Services, PO Box 269,
Abingdon, Oxon, OX14 4YN, UK
Tel: +44 (0)1235 465500
Fax: +44 (0)1235 465556
Email: direct.orders@marston.co.uk

In the USA and Canada:
ISBS, 920 NE 58th Street, Suite 300,
Portland, OR 97213-3786, USA
Tel: +1 800 944 6190 (toll free)
Fax: +1 503 280 8832
Email: info@isbs.com

In Australia and New Zealand:
DA Information Services, 648 Whitehorse Road
Mitcham, Victoria 3132, Australia
Tel: +61 (3) 9210 7777
Fax: +61 (3) 9210 7788
E-mail: service@dadirect.com.au

Further information about all of our titles can be found on our website: **www.policypress.org.uk**